THE CHANGING FA

St Clements
and East Oxford

BOOK TWO

Susanne Shatford
and
Trevor Williams

Robert Boyd
PUBLICATIONS

Published by
Robert Boyd Publications
260 Colwell Drive
Witney, Oxfordshire OX8 7LW

First published 1998

Copyright © Susanne Shatford, Trevor Williams and
Robert Boyd Publications

ISBN: 1 899536 19 1

OTHER TITLES IN THE *CHANGING FACES* SERIES

Banbury: Book One
Bladon with Church Hanborough and Long Hanborough
Botley and North Hinksey
Cowley
Cowley: Book Two
Cumnor and Appleton with Farmoor and Eaton
St Clements and East Oxford: Book One
Eynsham: Book One
Headington: Book One
Headington: Book Two
Jericho: Book One
Littlemore and Sandford
Marston: Book One
Marston: Book Two
North Oxford: Book One
Summertown and Cutteslowe
St Ebbes and St Thomas: Book One
St Ebbes and St Thomas: Book Two
Wolvercote with Wytham and Godstow
Woodstock: Book One
Woodstock: Book Two

FORTHCOMING

Bicester: Book One
Cowley: Book Three
Cowley Works
Eynsham: Book Two
Faringdon and District
Jericho: Book Two
North Oxford: Book Two
Oxford City Centre: Book One
South Oxford
Thame
Witney: Book One
West Oxford

Printed and bound in Great Britain at The Alden Press, Oxford

Contents

Cover illustrations

Front: A drama production c1900. The performance is believed
to have taken place at either SS. Mary and John School
or Church Hall. Lucy Jeffery is seated 1st on the left.

Back: Children and St. Clement's infant school in 1930s.

Acknowledgements

We would like to thank the following for there generous contributions, without which we would not have been able to produce this book (and our apologies to anyone we have inadvertently omitted from the list):

Hazel Anderson
Dennis Banton
Brian & Diana Battrick
John Blakeman
Roger & Vera Bradley
Majorie Bristow
Jean Chilton
Angela Craft
Kathleen Dean
Una Dean
Bob Duke
Colin Gammon
Rosa Gooderham
Rosemary & John Gray
Bill Hainge
Eric Harris
Ron Harris
Bob Haynes
Barbara Izzard
Doreen King

Rosemary & David Ledger
Heather MacDonald
Jane Madden
Maureen Mannion
Ada McCabe
Sheila McGuinness
Jack Moss
Gordon Oswell
Michael Pargeter
R.A.Porter
Mrs Quartermain
Dr M Raynor
Mary Reeve
John Scoble
Ron Shepherd
Bernard Slater
Leslie Smith
Thelma Telling
Joan and Don Timms
Emily Wakefield

East Oxford Liberal Club
East Oxford Bowls Club
Jeremys P.C., Oxford Stamp Centre
Brian Martin, Magdalen College School
Colin Harris, Bodleian Library
M.M. McCormack, St Josephs School
Paul Freestone, Photographer, Circus Workshop, Cowley Road
John Kirby, Scout Museum
Diana Shaw, Milham Ford School
Elizabeth Boardman, Archivist, St, Hildas College, Oriel College
Adrian Shatford for maps and drawings
Margaret Cullen
Wendy Williams for collating information

Preface

'What is this life if full of care?
We have no time to stand and stare.'
(W.H. Davies)

Whilst browsing through St Clement's and East Oxford Book 1, it was good to discover that so many people had done just that. What an interesting and varied recollection of past days and people. I was enabled as, I am sure so many others have done, to relive some happy times. And now here are some more — I hope these further memories will give as much pleasure to their readers, as they have done to those of us privileged to contribute to them.   Marjorie Bristow February 1998.

This second volume on St Clement's and East Oxford seeks to supplement, extend and in some places clarify the information in the first book. We are dependent on and eternally grateful to all those enthusiastic contributors, who have lent us their photographs and shared their memories. Without them these *'trips down memory lane'* would be impossible. Please note that we have not classified material strictly according to parish and therefore, some St Clement's photographs have been included in the East Oxford section, where they relate more logically to the Cowley Road. Also note that photograghs are named from left to right unless otherwise stated.

Arthur Place off Caroline Street, showing a typical terrace of houses where the poorer members of St Clement's resided at the beginning of this century. Note the two little girls without shoes, a very common sight at that time. (*Bodleian Library Oxford. Minn Collection 8/81*)

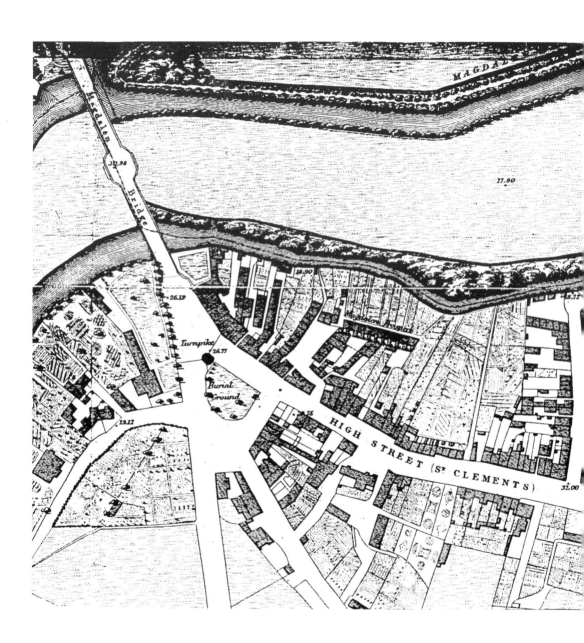

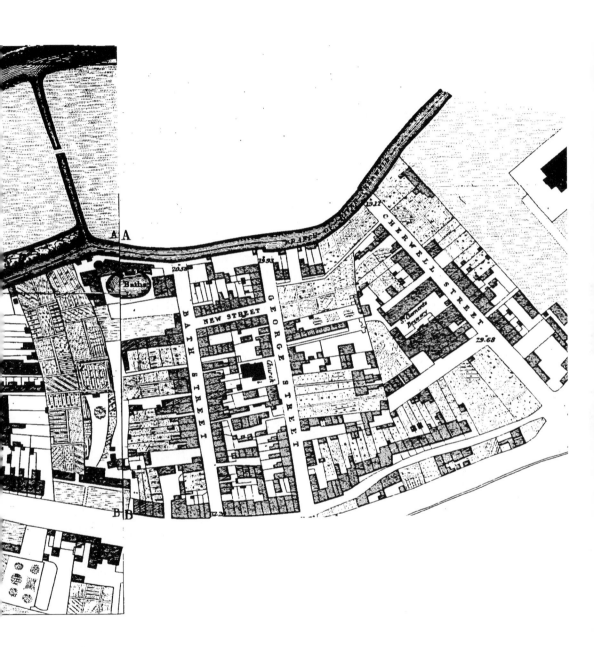

A map of St Clement's by Hoggar in 1850.

Part One: St Clements

SECTION ONE

Cowley Place

Magdalen College School

In 1480, William Waynfleet founded Magdalen College and shortly after, he started to build a grammar school within the college grounds. The first schoolroom was a vaulted chamber below the Chapel of St John's Hospital, which stood between the porter's lodge and the tower. In 1851, a new schoolroom was designed by John Buckler and opened on the corner of Long Wall and now houses the college library.

Under the leadership of J.E. Millard, Master from 1846-64, the school expanded from 18 pupils to 68 boarders and 28 day boys. However its popularity was not sustained and in 1888, when W.E. Sherwood, a former pupil under Millard, became Master, it was in danger of collapsing. He worked hard to revitalise the school and by 1897 there were 100 pupils. As recognition of Sherwood's leadership, a new boarding house was built to replace the dilapidated accommodation in Long Wall. The ground was leased from Christ Church College and the playing field was in use for football by the winter of 1894/95, even though the players had to be punted across the river initially, until the bridges were built. This site, which lies on the banks of the Cherwell is probably the most beautiful in Oxford, despite its liability to flood.

The school has always tried to bridge the gap between the University and the City, and has admitted boys from a wide variety of backgrounds. In the 1920s, when the school became partially under the management of the Board of Education, scholarship boys from the City were given access to the Public School System. Consequently the school grew and in 1928 it removed to the west-side of Iffley Road and occupied temporary buildings on the corner of Cowley Place. In the 1940s it became a direct-grant- school and gained independent status in 1976.

Magdalen College School House built for the boarders in 1893. The college choristers have been boarders since the 15th century.

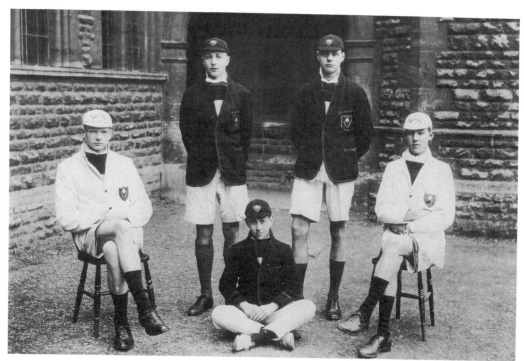

Magdalen College School 1st rowing IV in 1925. Back row: B.J. Rushby-Smith (3). 11. 5. H.L.O. Rees (bow). 10.3. Front row: M.B. Higgins (stroke and Captain). 10.2. C.I.F. Mackay. (Cox) 7. W.A. Ebbutt (2, Hon. Sec). 11.3.

The school buildings on the south side of Cowley Place in 1958. From left to right they house the laboratories, the library and Big School flanked by teaching rooms.

In 1928, the College took over the schoolroom within its grounds, and plans for new buildings on the west side of the Iffley Road, were drawn up by Sir Giles Gilbert Scott. However the design proved too expensive and a cheaper, but equally useful building was erected.

An Upper Sixth group in the senior laboratory in 1958. On the left is S.M. Lloyd-Williams with B.E. Mash, G.C. Pye and D.J. Haviald on the front bench.

A class at work in 1958. Far back: G.C. Cox. 4th row: R.A. Boulger, B.J. Daube, –, –. 3rd row: C.J.Beesley, G.D. Carson, J. Hancock, –. 2nd row: J.L. Bielby, A. Hawkins, A.A. Brown, T.J. Dennis. Front: N.G.J. Holder, G.G. Innes, –, S.C.O. Kestner.

Milham Ford School

Milham Ford started its life as a nursery school at 7a and 8a Iffley Road. It was opened by two sisters, Emma and Jane Moody in the parlour of their parents home where they taught the children of friends and acquaintances. They were not formally qualified but were *'accomplished, musical and devout'* and therefore very suited to working with young children. By 1900 the school had grown and moved to a small house in Cowley Place near to the old ford across the Cherwell, from which the school took its name.

The Misses Moody with their pupils in 1903; girls of all ages appear to have been admitted with a few younger boys. Back row from left: 5th Dorothy Houghton, 6th a teacher, 7th Miss Emma Moody. 4th row: Miss McDonald (teacher), 3rd — Wiltshire, 5th — Ford, right Miss Evans? 3rd row: 5th — Slaughter. 2nd row: 6th Miss Jane Moody, Right — Ford. Front row: 2nd Theodore Ford, 5th — Ford, 7th Gertie Timbs, 10th Gordon —, 11th John Timbs, 12th Gilbert Hunt.

In 1904 the school was bought by the Church Education Corporation, which was committed to encouraging the education of girls. Miss Catherine Dodd was appointed as Headmistress and managed both the school and the adjoining teacher training college for women graduates called Cherwell Hall. The Church Education Corporation had become aware of the need for properly trained teachers and as Milham Ford had been recognised as efficient by the Board of Education, a working partnership developed between the school and the college.

The new School 1906

A new purpose-built school was opened in 1906 by the Right Honourable Augustine Birrell, Minister of Education. This building is now incorporated into St Hilda's College. The numbers of pupils increased and several temporary classrooms, known as the 'huts' were erected around the main building.

Pupils old and young cultivating their allotments during World War 1. The main school can be seen on the right. The allotments ceased to exist by 1920.

The staff in October 1924. All were well qualified single ladies. Note the long length of service of many members of staff.

Back row	Years of Service	Subject
Frances Mountain	1923-26	Science
Gwendoline Fry	1924-	Art, English
Clarice Nicholson	1922–	French
Winifred Bartrop	1922-55	French, English, Latin
Ursula Thompson	1921-55	History
Olive Fontaine	1919-46	Needlework
Sibyll Mayall	1921-27	French

Front row	Years of Service	Subject
Christine Wiblin	1919-29	Music
Margaret Powell	1922-25	Geography
Marion Davies	1918-28	Maths, Science
Annie Edwards	1908-33	Classics, English
Joan McCabe OBE	**1912- 1931**	**Headmistress**
Margaret Overend	1921-53	Botany
Annie McMeikan	1921-58	Mathematics
Winifred Earle	1922-53	English
Violet Blockley	1921-26	Secretary

The fifth form in 1924.

Back row: Phyllis Cole, Winnie McDonald, Dorothea Ducker, –, Kathleen Carmody, Violet Townsend, Rene Weller, –. Middle row: –, –, –, Mary Potter, Miss Nicholson, Molly Axtell, Lois Watts, Doreen –, Violet Marshall. Front row: Betty Gray, –, –, –.

Olive Cox, later to become Olive Gibbs pictured on the right of the front row in the summer of her final year at Milham Ford.

Over the years the uniform changed considerably. In 1903, their were no apparent regulations, but by the 1920s, girls of all ages were wearing white long sleeved blouses, black or navy gym slips with white belts and black stockings. The straw boaters, commonly known as 'bashers' were part of the summer uniform and clearly identified pupils. The girl on the left is wearing the standard blue hat band and the one on the right, has the striped band of the school prefects. Bashers ceased to be worn when the school lost its grammar school status.

St. Hilda's College

Miss Dorothea Beale, Principal of Cheltenham Ladies College, founded St Hilda's in 1893 as a house where her students and teachers could avail themselves of the University facilities. She aimed to provide an opportunity for study unrelated to examinations, and reading courses appertaining to individual needs. She purchased Cowley House in 1892 for £5,000 from Dr G.W. Child. The house had been built between 1775 and 1783 for Dr Humphrey Sibthorpe, Sherardian Professor of Botany, on the foundations of an older house. Miss Beale appointed Mrs Esther Elizabeth Burrows, a member of the Bliss family, who owned the Tweed Mill at Chipping Norton, as Principal. She had previously been in charge of one of the Cheltenham private boarding houses and was 'socially suitable'.

In 1897 the establishment was formally registered as St Hilda's Hall Incorporated; a new wing was added and by 1900 there were 20 students. Miss Beale died in 1906 but the Hall continued to grow and in 1921, the lease on Cherwell Hall was purchased. This followed the University's acceptance of women in June 1920. Women students could now be matriculated and gained undergraduate status. In 1926 a royal charter was granted, St Hilda's Incoporated College was disbanded and St Hilda's, Oxford was born.

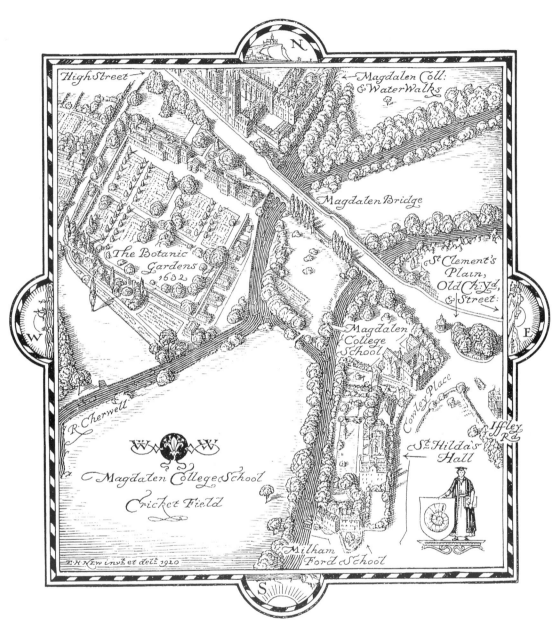

'AS FOR OUTLODGINGS (LIKE GALLERIES, NECESSARY
EVILS IN POPULOUS CHURCHES), THE GOOD MASTER OF
A COLLEDGE RATHER TOLERATES THAN APPROVES THEM.'
Fuller, '*The Holy State.*'

Cowley Place by T.H. New 1920.

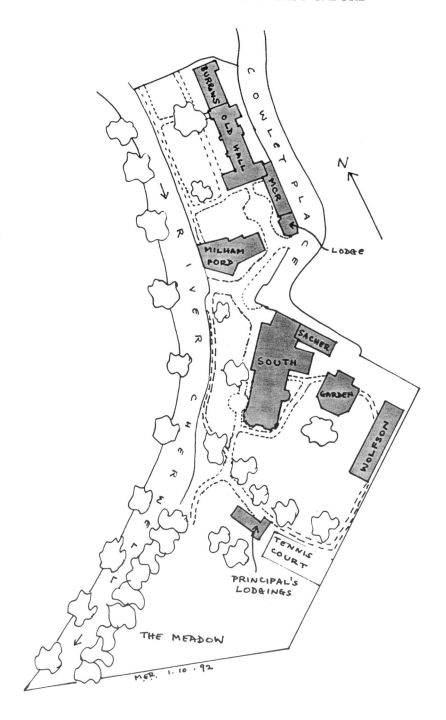

St Hilda's College Campus in 1992, showing how the college has expanded to include the Milham Ford School building and Cowley House, which formed the nucleus of the old building and became known as St Hilda's Hall. Cherwell Hall was adapted for student accommodation and became known as St Hilda's South. (*Reproduced by kind permission of Dr M. E. Rayner.*)

Schools

St Clement's School

The school seems to have started its life in George Street (now Cave Street) in the Baptist Chapel. This chapel had been built in 1824 with James Hinton as its minister. He worked along side Father Newman at the Anglican Church to combat the irreligious attitudes of the community. The chapel had cost £750 to build and unfortunately the debt still remained at £600 in 1836. As the congregation was unable to meet the expense, the building was put up for sale and was purchased in 1839 by the rector and churchwardens for £525. It was converted into a free school and was aided by an annual endowment of £20 from the Dawson Trust. By 1854, about 200 boys, girls and infants attended the school. The building was demolished in 1949 and the remains of coffins and bones were found on the site. This caused great speculation among the residents, who did not know the origins of the site.

In 1891 a new Girls School was built in Boulter Street for 204 pupils while the boys moved to Cross Street in 1903. The Girls School closed in 1929 and the Cross Street premises expanded to serve both boys and girls of all ages.

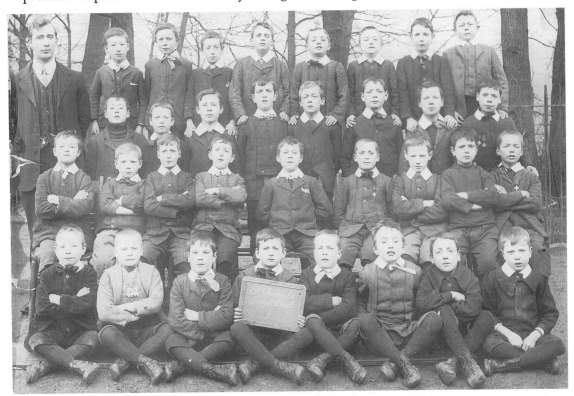

St Clement's Boys School c1904. In the back row 5th from the left is George Hayward from George Street (now Cave Street). Note the medals which were issued for good attendance and punctuality.

St Clement's Girls School in Boulter Street c1905. Back row 2nd from left is Gladys Hopkins. In the 3rd row, 2nd from the right is Ruth Bristow with Kathie Bristow on the far right in the second row.

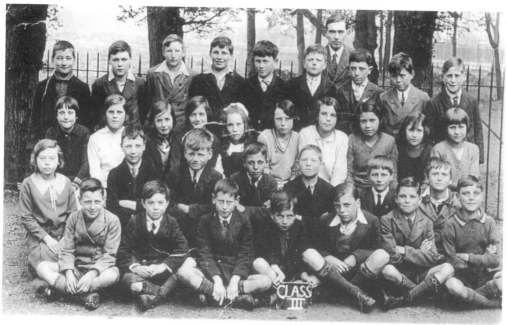

Class III St Clement's School in 1930. Back row: S. Phipps, –, M. Richens, J Curtis, T. Rogers, H. Green, –, –, K. Cullimore. 3rd row: –, Edna Wallin, Joan Bare, Lucy Galloway, Rosemary Harris, Gladys Bolton, –, Ena Lee, Ruby Hornsby, Jean Stone. 2nd row: Joan Goodwin, Les Green, Mick Evans, Jim Brown, A. Waite, Bill Taylor, M. Allen. Front row: –, S. Simms, C. Collier, L. Robbins, L. Brooks, Ron Strange, –.

Class I in 1931. Back row: Mr Jones, Charlie Butt, Mick Evans, Doug Stowell, Alf Adams, Ron Shepherd, Miss Jellis. Middle row: Norah Harris, Barbara Palfrey, Iris Stone, Barbara Cook, –, Eileen Harris, Gladys Stockford, Joyce Kilby. Front row: Maurice Richings, – Hornsby, Frank Thornett, George Sadler, Jim Brown, – Bayliss.

St Clement's School football team in 1931. Back row: Mr Jones, Mr Spiller. 3rd row: W. Evans, B. Taylor, A. Waite, H. Wallin, – Harris, B. Acaster. 2nd row: S. Strange, J North, K. Cullimore, Ron Strange, N. Coon, R. Green, C. Ramsden. Front row: R. Harris, S. Simms, K. Walker, R. Mansel, K. Brooks, –.

St Joseph's Roman Catholic School, St Clement's.

The chapel of St Ignatius was erected between 1793 and 1806 and the burial ground was consecrated in 1798. It was initiated by Father Charles Leslie of the Society of Jesus, who had been appointed to the mission at Waterperry. However there were so few Catholics in the vicinity that, in 1790 he decided to move the mission to Oxford. It is alleged that he chose St Clement's as there was a Roman Catholic tradition in the area and land outside the city was cheaper. Parishioners were drawn from all over the county but only numbered 160 and in 1804, as the walls reached a height of about twenty feet, the building fund ran into difficulties. Moneys were being directed to support the French Revolution and Father Leslie, after appealing to his congregation, was forced to lend money to complete the building. He writes at this time that his congregation, *'has not in its power to repay me the capital I have advanced nor the interest thereof. For though they are about 160 in number, still there is scarcely a person of any property amongst them, so that the bench money scarcely pays for the wine and candles at the altar ...'.*

Father Leslie died suddenly on 28th December 1806 and was buried in front of the pulpit in the chapel. He was commemorated by a brass plate saying, *'By his amiable manner and classical attainments he conciliated the respect and the esteem of many members of the University'.* His elder brother, Father James Leslie succeeded him and served until 1812.

Leslie House was the home of the Parish Priest and in the late 1840s both Rev. John Newman and Father Dominic Barberi were frequent visitors. The chapel can be seen on the right *'a solemn and handsome edifice decorated in a style of elegant simplicity'* which remained in dual use as a school and Mass Centre, after the completion of the new church of St Aloysius in St Giles, in 1875.

The St Aloysius Roman Catholic School was opened on 4 October 1869 with Anne Norah Slattery as the teacher in charge. However there appears to have been a school on the premises before this date as the 1869 logbook refers to the school as St Aloysius, formerly St Ignatius School. In 1908 it became St Aloysius Girls and Infants as the boys school was situated at the rear of St Aloysius Church in St Giles. In the early 1930s the city Catholic Schools were reorganised and the St Clement's site became known as St Joseph's Mixed and Infants. In 1947, the senior department became St Joseph's Secondary Modern School.

In 1909 Leslie House was demolished and was replaced by a new school building consisting of three classrooms and cloakrooms. The picture above was taken in 1957. Outside are three of the older pupils: Donald Horne who died in 1983, is seen talking to Neil Saunders and Paddy Franklin on bicycles.

A Class in 1932 when St Joseph's included boys beyond the infant age. Included in the front row standing are: 1st Frances Cartwright, 4th Gwen Turley, 6th Avis Baker.

The Chorus in a school production in 1946. The group are upper seniors aged 14 years. Back row: Stanley Clapton, Brian Mills. 3rd row: – Borg, –, Margaret Bourton, Mary O'Hara, Janet Butlin. 2nd Row: Pamela Evans, Nan O'Hara, –, Yvonne Paintin, – Sheenan, Ann Wyatt. Front row: Nora McTieran, Nancy Lee, Nancy Hornsby, Eileen Cornhill.

Mr. Pat Reynolds Class in 1946. Back row: Mary Carroll, Amelia Long, Margaret McLoughlan, Cecilia Hannon, Margaret Bernie, Margaret Flanagan, Rita Borg, Maria Borg, Ann O'Hara, –, -Brogan, –. Front row: –, Dennis Neeson, –, Kathleen Ward, Teresa Martin, Rosemary Bates, Ann McDade, – McDermott, Danny Buckley, Paddy Pancott, Rosemary Alder, – O'Connor.

The May Procession outside St Edmund and St Frideswide Church on the Iffley Road in 1947. The May Queen is Betty Doyle and she is attended by Marjorie Mould (crown bearer), Ellen Franklin and Patsy Cleary (train bearers), and Pat Murphy (centre front), Olive Stone, Evelyn Baker and Helen Hannoway? The participants were the previous year's first Holy Communicants and they crowned the statue of Our Lady in the Church.

The Corpus Christi Procession in Stratford Street.

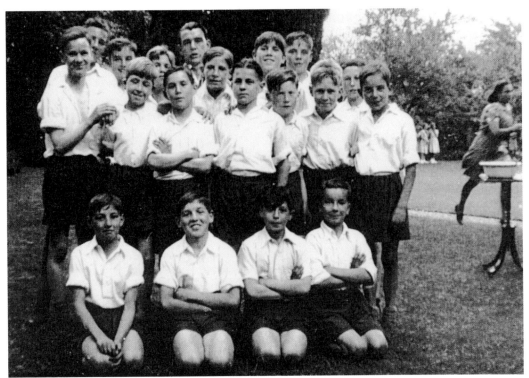

A group enjoying Sports Day in July 1940. Back row: Cecil Mobey, Maurice McAvoy, –, –, Mr Murray, –, Leonard Butler, – Mills. Middle row: – Harvey, – Dalaway, – Rocha, – Fletcher, – Lee, Tom Gleeson, Edwin Bourton. Front row: Ivor Hawkins, – Franklin, Vincent Villa, Bernard Mobey.

St Joseph's football team c.1942. From the left: Ian Weygang (died in an accident in 1950s), Walter Horn, –, –, –, – Dalloway, – Swanson, Stanley Clapton, Peter Weygang, –, – Salter.

The Electrons were an after school club and this was a group taken in 1946. Back row: Greta Shields, Kathleen Lavelle, Mary Robinson. Fourth row: –, Olive Stone, Nan O'Hare, –. Third row: Nancy Lee, Margo Bowen, Maureen Thomas, Jean Collins, Eileen Cornhill. Second row: Doreen Crawford, Patsy Long, Ann Wyatt, –. Front row: –, Margaret Bourton, Diana Hale, Audrey Mould, Chrissie Spicer, Yvonne Painton, –.

The school staff in 1958 before the school moved. Back row: Philip Powley (Headteacher), Shelagh Walsh, Susan Parrott. Middle row: Monica Stokes, Maria Beaton, Norah Palmer, Kathleen Bedlington, Betty Enwright, Mrs Rhodes, Odile Bloice, Ena Cripps. Front row: George Lunt, Paul Stiven, Father Lake, Frank Taylor, Patrick Hughes.

The school closed in 1958 and the primary children moved to a new building on Headley Way in July 1959; the secondary children went to Edmund Campion School. During the reorganisation the Infants were accommodated in Catherine Street

St Joseph's Scouts.

The 17th Oxford Scout Group based at St Joseph's School pictured c.1955 on an exchange visit to Bensberg near Cologne. Back row: R. Stoker, R. Mallet, A. Moran, J. Etherington, R. King, M. Bires, J Jordan, J. Creed, M. Sweeney. Middle row: W. Parker, O. Mew, P. Bartlett, M. Duhig, P. Powley, M. Powley, Herr Wagner (Town Clerk) P. Franklin. Front row: J. Malley, P. Stokes, R. Kimber, J. Friel, M. Wade, K. Mulcahy.

17th Oxford Scouts at Lands End c. 1958. Back row: D. Skinner, J. Dalton P. O'Brien, W. Parker. 3rd row: D. Mew, R. Cleary, M. Jones D. Paul, J. Creed, L. Cuddy, R. McCann, D. Breen, −, D. Smith, J. Malley, Bartlett. M. Wide, P. Franklin, P. Powley, J.Friel. 2nd row: L. King, V. Coughlan, R. McAvey, P. Mulvany,, T. Franklin, P. O'Neal, A. Moran, D. Batten, − Bolton, C. Beckinsale, J. Etherington, P. McKenzie. Front row: P. McKiernan, G. King, M. O'Donnell, R. Dell, D. Wilson, D. Smith, P. West, K. Barnes.

Nazareth House

Nazareth House was situated on a 3 acre site at the junction of Cowley road and Rectory Road, formerly Pembroke Street. The building was originally an elegant private house known as 'Charnwood Lodge' and in 1875 was purchased by the Congregation of the Poor Sisters of Nazareth.

In 1850, the first Catholic Archbishop of Westminster, Dr Wiseman, was appointed and he recognised the need to care both for the elderly and for the orphaned poor. He contacted a newly established order in France and was sent three sisters, who were to form the nucleus of the Poor Sisters of Nazareth. The order based its philosophy on the Holy Family of Nazareth and set out to provide homes 'full of peace and happiness'.

The first Mother General of the new Congregation was Mother St Basil, born Victoire Larmenier. The order was established in Hammersmith in 1855 and vows were taken to establish homes for poor and orphaned children throughout the U.K. They would all be called Nazareth House and the Mother House would remain in Hammersmith. By the time of Mother St Basil's death in 1878, she had seen eight houses established across the country, one of which was at Oxford.

Mother St Basil

The 'Parlour' purchased in 1875 and renamed 'Larminier House' after Mother St Basil. It was extended in 1876 to provide a kitchen, refectory and offices at ground level with a chapel above. In 1878 a stable block with common room and first floor bedrooms was added and c.1900 a new detached wing named after the architect, Edward Goldie was completed. The Goldie Wing was converted into a nursing home for the elderly with 6 bedrooms on each floor and a lift for access, when the need to cater for children ceased. Nazareth House finally closed in 1995 and was bought by Oriel College.

The girls were educated in the convent classroom until 1925, when according to the St Joseph's School logbook, 28 girls were admitted from Nazareth House as the sisters had given up their own school.

The children of Nazareth House in Cowley Road c.1955. Back row: Maureen Mannion, Anne Clancy, Father Marcellus, Kathleen Wright, Jean Mold. Middle row: Gillian Latimer, Anne Leonard, Sister Providence, –. Front row: Anita Pearson, Carol McClerk, Angela Demarco, Pauline Guinan, Patricia Banks, Margaret Delaney, Teresa Murphy, Sally Ann Hilton, Patricia O'Neil, Teresa Martin. Very front row: Miriam Best, Margaret Miller.

Joan, Christine and Francesco O'Brian in the Convent garden in 1961.

Angela Demarco remembers life at the Convent in the 1950s.

'*There were around thirty five girls in the Convent for various reasons i.e. parents couldn't cope, children of unmarried mums, children who had lost a parent and of course, orphans.*

Some parents would come and take their children out for the day, or on holiday with them. In the playground there was a climbing frame. Miriam, Patsy, two others and myself used to climb to the top of it and sit and watch them go, with tears streaming down our faces wishing it were us and our parents. It was so unfair!'

Angela Demarco and Maureen Mannion remember well the routine of Convent life.

Life in the Convent seemed to centre around praying, cleaning and washing. There was a strict routine which allowed no freedom of thought or action.

On Wednesdays, Fridays and Sundays we were woken up early to go to Mass in the chapel, but on the other days we stayed in bed a little longer. On rising we knelt by our beds and prayed. We then went to the washroom — washing was a difficult task as we had to keep a towel tucked under our arms to cover our chests. Baths were on Wednesdays and Saturdays and we had to wear a bath slip (like a hospital gown) in the bath as it was considered indecent to be naked even when alone. Jeyes fluid was added to the bath water so it always looked dirty!

After dressing, we had to air our beds; we stripped the bed clothes off, turned the mattresses and laid our blankets at the foot of our beds. Breakfast followed; we were always well fed- scrambled eggs, bacon etc. We then made our beds and went to the schoolroom, where we knelt to say the rosary.

The Convent was always kept clean and tidy in case visitors arrived. Each morning the cleaning had to be done before school. We all had chores to do; some worked in the kitchens, others in the laundry, some scrubbed corridors or cleaned the dormitories and bathrooms. Angela remembers cleaning the chapel, dusting and trimming the candles after mass. When tasks were completed satisfactorily, we went to school; an older girl accompanied us.

Here are a group of us leaving for school in 1956. Back row: Yvonne Law, Kathleen (a senior girl supervisor), Angela Demarco, Maureen Mannion, Kathleen Wright. Front row: —, —, Pat Banks, —, Miriam (Minnie) Best.

We attended St Joseph's in St Clement's, but we were nearly always late through no fault of our own and ended up in Mother Honoria's office to receive the cane on our hands — very painful! At lunch-time we returned to the Convent for a good hot dinner. After school we returned to more cleaning. We had tea, then, changed out of our school clothes. Angela remembers having to clean all the children's shoes for school next day — the line seemed never ending to a seven year old. Maureen remembers polishing the floors with rags tied to her feet; a line of girls would progress up the hall or dormitory in unison, left, right. Maureen remembers it clearly as she was hit with a broom for not keeping in step.

Clothes were paid for with money donated by the local community. On Sundays we wore fairisle jumpers with matching hats and pleated skirts. Maureen also remembers that each child had a number; she was number 27.

On Wednesdays, Fridays and Sundays we attended Benediction in the chapel.
When the chores were over, we were sent to play or watch the television that the American soldiers had given to us. We ate supper and on really cold nights when the dormitories were freezing, we were given hot soup or gruel before bed-time to keep us warm. We knelt beside our beds to say our prayers and everyone was in bed before 9 p.m. Maureen remembers having to sleep on her back, her arms folded across her chest. with legs together. It was thought that if we died in the night, we would be ready for the coffin!

Holidays were exchange visits to other Convents across the country and we had lots of enjoyable visits to parties at the American air bases; they were very generous and gave us chocolate and cereal bars. They also provided the outdoor play equipment – a climbing frame and roundabout.

The main entrance to the Convent taken in 1995. The white building is a recent addition but in the 1960s the building on the left was for the elderly, the main chapel on the first floor was over the sewing room and the Nuns chapel and refectory was on the right. Just in view (right) is the original house where the Nuns lived known as the Parlour. At the rear was a mortuary which the girls referred to as the 'Dead House'.

Life story by Maureen Mannion:

The large flat ground where I sat and watched them play was cut in half by a long green hedge. The nuns, dressed in black, rimmed with dark blue down to their feet; walked, talked and prayed. They seemed to hide from us under their shrouds.

The ground was harsh and cold. Stones were used to mark the ground to play a game of squares. Steel poles made a frame where we could climb and play. The top of the high bus soared past the high wall. A face peered down at us! What went on in that world out there?

First Holy Communion Group in 1950 taken on the Parlour steps. Back row: Anne Leonard, Maureen Mannion, —. Middle row: Kathleen Wright, Anne Clancy. Front row: Yvonne Law, Patricia O'Neal, —. Very front: Monica Williams.

The crowning of our Lady, May 1952.

Maureen Mannion is crowning the statue of Our Lady in the Convent garden. Angela Demarco can be seen in the background in the centre of the three attendants; Jean Mold and Pauline Guinan were flower attendants. The May Queen and attendants were the previous year's first holy communicants. The girls really enjoyed the processions as they loved to sing.

Angela Craft (nee Demarco) standing outside the front door beneath the statue of the Sacred Heart of Jesus, just after the Convent closed on 5 September 1995. Angela remembers seeing this statue in her dreams.

A reunion of Nazareth House girls with family and friends 29 September 1987. Back row: Tony Heeley, Ann Gates, Betty Swanton, Teresa Martin,★ Pat Hayes, Yvonne Paintin, Annie Lambell,★ Eileen Cornhill, Betty Doyle, Betty Ayres. Middle: Mrs Rene Williams, Mr Jim Williams, Agnes Mary Walton,★ Rose Hamblin, Yvonne Law.★ Front row: Stan Bowler, Josephine O'Hare,★ Ena Chandler,★ Eileen Aldridge, Bunty Matthews.

★ indicates those girls who grew up in the Convent.

Civil Defence Messengers

The Messengers were part of a national network which was organised to carry messages in times of crisis.

The St Clement's Civil Defence Messengers taken c. 1943 in the garden, at the back of their premises on the Plain. The building now houses the Y.H.A. shop. Back row: D. Clarke, 4th D. Parker. 3rd row: 7th D. Haggis, 8th I. Smith, 11th R. Croxon, right F. Gomm (sailor). 2nd row: 4th P. Wade, 5th Group Leader Ms Perkins O.B.E. Front row: 4th B. Little, 7th K. Cartwright.

The Oxford Marathon Rugby Football Club originated in the Civil Defence Youth Club. They are pictured above c.1949 participating in the Lord Mayor's Parade. The giant rugby ball has the names of their opponents. The club was based in the Civil Defence Club but later moved its headquarters to the Coach and Horses. The players pictured above are from the left: M. Taylor, B. Haynes, D. Parker, G. Mandle, J. Court and N. Dorn.

Oxford Marathon R.F.C. on South Park 1958/59. Far back row: John Filmer. Back row: Bob Haynes, –, –, –, –. Standing: Malcolm Davies –, –, Reggie Roberts, –, –, –, Idris Storrie, Roger Dringle, – Edwards, Norman Dover, Ian Hazel, –, –, –, –, –, Mick Brown, Dick Parker. Seated: Len Green, Don Robinson, Keith Lee, –, –.

Church Lads Brigade

Ron and Henry Shepherd, 20 Caroline Street, c1928.

Left to right: Ron Shepherd, Alf Messenger, Arthur Deacon, summer camp, Exmouth, Devon c1934.

c1939 Middle row: Lou Stone, Ron Harris, George Butler, Albert Wright, –.

London Place

London Place showing Harpsichord Row.

Until 1929, there was a second row of properties opposite the houses that we now know as London Place. It is alleged to have been known as Harpsichord row because of the shape of the site. The road to London passed behind the properties and there was a footpath down the middle. Minn records that in the 18th century the area was mainly occupied by stables. Francis Guiden, who was postmaster at the New Inn and Mayor of Oxford in 1788, together with William Costar of the Angel both had stables there.

A view of Harpsichord Row in the 1920s showing South Park on the right and George Street (now Cave Street) on the left. The public house seen on the left is the Duke of Edinburgh and the establishment on the opposite corner of George Street, with the wooden steps leading up to the front door, was Edginton's Bakery. Mr Edginton provided an invaluable service to the community as families could get their Sunday dinners cooked for 2d, fruit cakes for 1½d. Dough cakes were great favourites and the dough was purchased from the Baker and the cake made at home; it was then returned to Edgington's to be baked.

The free-standing building in the centre of the picture with the white awning and the delivery van at the rear, was the Foreign Meat Shop. Cheap meat could be purchased here whereas those who preferred to 'buy British' went to Timbs further down St Clement's. (*Bodleian Library Oxford. M.S. Minn 8/37a*)

The entrance to London Place in 1910 with Harpsichord Row on the right.

No 4 on the left was a grocer's managed by the Villa family and on the right, with the wooden steps leading to the front door, was the pub called the Rising Sun.

No 6 with the railings in front was occupied by the Wright family in the 1920s. Mr Wright was blind and he earned his living as a woodman; he sold bundles of firewood which he chopped at the rear of the property. Mr and Mrs Wright lived here with their grand-daughter Ethel Waite. Mr Wright also bred rabbits to show.

Loder's second-hand shop can be seen in the distance. Butt's Dairy occupied the centre of the Row and milk could be purchased from the rear of the business on the London Road. (*Bodleian Library Oxford. M.S. Minn 31/2/7*)

The Headington end of Harpsichord Row showing Cherwell Street on the right. In the centre, in front of the lamp were two drinking troughs; the larger for horses and the smaller for dogs. Harpsichord Row was demolished in 1929 so that the road could be widened.

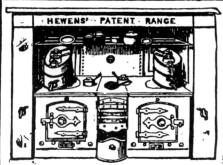

By her Majesty's Royal Letters Patent.

KITCHENERS.

TO allwho study ECONOMY.—Save HALF your COALS, and CURE your SMOKY CHIMNEYS, by using

HEWENS' IMPROVED LEAMINGTON KITCHENER,

Fitted with the PATENT REGULATOR, which will cook for a family at less cost than any apparatus yet invented; together with HEWENS' NEW CONVERTIBLE RANGE, with high-pressure boiler, comprising all the advantages of the Leamington Kitchener. The public are respectfully invited to inspect a large Stock at the DEPOT, 26, HIGH STREET, ST. CLEMENT'S, OXFORD.

N.B. R. HEWENS will fit the PATENT REGULATOR (see annexed engraving) to any of the old style of grates without removing them, at small cost. **Sole Agent for Oxford—Mr. JAMES TURBITT, at the Depot.**

An advertisement from the Oxford Chronicle & Bucks & Berks Gazette Saturday 21 December 1861.

LONDON PLACE (St. Clement's), from 76 St. Clement's street.

1 Edginton Albert, baker
2 Green Hubert, boot ma
3 Eeley William Henry
4 Spindler Fredk. confctr
4A. Rowe Samuel Mark
5 Hughes Mrs. Wm. laundry
6 Jarvis Bertie, beer retlr
7 Chaundy Ernest
8 Thomas Mrs
9 Chaundy Harry William
10 Birmingham Frederick
11 Richardson Edward
12 Ayres Mrs. Ann, university lodgings
13 Harvey Mrs. university lodgings
14 Raleigh Miss
15 Roberts John William
16 Tanner Mrs
17 Couling James

17 Fitt G. W. supt. of London, Edinburgh & Glasgow Assurance Co. Limited
18 Simpson Miss
19 Harvey Miss
20 Hunter Ernest Fredk
21 Udell George Edward
22 Whareham James Walter, tailor
23 Bateman Edward
24 Drury William
25 Connop Edward Leonard
26 Piper Henry Arthur
27 Harris Walter
28 Payne George, confectnr
.........here are Cherwell st. Marston rd. & Headington hill......................
28 Lee Frederick Charles
29 Loder George, watchma

30 O'Neill Mrs. confectionr
31 Boflin Mrs
32 Brimfield Percival Frank
33 Russell James
34 Stroudley Mrs
35 & 36 Brooks Sl. dairyman
37 Hedges Charles & Son, monumental sculptors
38 Carter Alfred
39 Nash William John
40 Sturges Mrs. Eliza, beer retailer
41 Davis Stephen
  Premier Meat Co. (The)
... here is St. Clement's st ...

London & North Western Coal wharf.
See REWLEY ROAD.

The residents of London Place and Harpsichord Row in 1910. (*courtesy of Reed Information Systems*)

The Oxford Asphalt Co. were based in the house to the left of 'Ferndale' pictured on the next page.

'Ferndale' now No 78 St Clement's, which faces Cave Street, pictured c.1909. Kate Wakefield, who was in the service of Mrs Stevens is standing on the steps.

This row of houses hit the headlines c1940 when the occupant, a Miss Kempson was murdered by her lodger. The Kempsons kept a good class green grocers on the corner of Pensions Gardens.

South Park occupies 50 acres of land between Headington Hill and Morrell Avenue. It belonged to the Morrell family of brewers, who owned Headington Hill Hall from 1831-1953. In 1932 it was acquired by the Oxford Preservation Trust. Eric Gill's monument at the bottom of Headington Hill, facing London Place, commemorates the contributions of the Pilgrim Trust, which was a forerunner of the English Heritage, and David and Joanna Randall McIver.

The Trust gave the park to the City Council in 1959 to be preserved for the use of the public.

Shops and Businesses

Sidney H. Oswell, Antique and Modern Furniture Dealer.

Sidney Oswell came to Oxford in the 1920s from Birmingham, where he had worked as an upholsterer for Daimler, before becoming a charge-hand for Austin Motors. He took up a position at Pressed Steel but soon left to set up his own upholstery business in Old High Street, Headington. In 1934, he moved down the hill to No. 27 St Clement's, where he was joined in the business by his son Gordon in the early 1960s. Gordon Oswell operated from two premises until the 1980s and continues to trade at Nos 103/104 as the Oxford Gas Log Fire Studio, which he established in 1979. The family have now completed 64 years and are the longest serving members of the business community still in existence.

Sidney Oswell 1880-1966 pictured here in the 1950s.

The furniture shop photographed by Paul Freestone in October 1980. This building was situated next to the St. Clement's car park, with its front on the pavement. It had originally been a farmhouse, which faced up towards Headington Hill with land going down to the banks of the Cherwell. In the 1980s, the property together with No 28 next-door, was sold by the City Council to the Oxford Buildings Trust for £3,000. They completed the renovations and sold the building to Greytown Properties Ltd for £210,000; the property agency Finders Keepers now occupies the premises. Gordon Oswell was brought up over this shop.

The Oswell brothers in 1942 feeding the swans by the Cherwell behind their property. They are standing on the landing stage of the boat yard. Eric is on the left and Gordon is watching on the right.

In 1936 Nos 27 and 28 caught fire and crowds gathered to watch the Fire Brigade in action. The pub on the right of Raja Products has now been set back from the road.

On the 4th June 1980, this car crashed into Oswell's premises and demolished the corner of the building. The premises were out of action for about a year.

Gordon Oswell pictured in his present shop at 103 St Clements, known as the Gas Log Fire Studio.

A.C. Haynes, Tobacconist and Newsagent

Alfred Haynes was born in Suffolk in 1906 and came to Oxford just after World War 1. He played football for his school, St Frideswides and after leaving played for the local side. He then transferred to Oxford City Football Club for two years and went on to play for Arsenal. In 1935 he was injured and had to retire, so he took over the newsagents business in St Clements from Mr Symes and managed it with his wife Ernestine (known as Ene) until 1960. Next door to Alf Haynes was a cobbler by the name of Bryan, who also dealt in horse equipment.

Nos 106 and 107 St Clements being demolished in 1966. The pedestrian crossing ran up to Haynes front door. No 108 had been used by the A.R.P. warden during the war, and afterwards became the Civil Defence Club.

Harry Slater, Fishmonger and Poulterer.

The No 1 bus which travelled from the Lamp in Hockmore Street, Cowley to Oxford Station is seen here at the Plain with Harry Slater's Fish and Poultry Shop in the background c1950.

Harry Slater's Fish Shop in Oxford Fish Week c1952. where Leslie Rhymes can be seen serving two customers. Mr Rhymes had been trained by Harry Slater before the war and after serving time in the navy, he returned to work in the business until it closed in March 1983.

Harry Slater was born in the City of London and learned his trade with George Smithers of Cannon Street, a fashionable London Fishmonger.

After completing his training, he removed to Reading where he was a branch manager for Colebrookes in Pangbourne, Berks. He came to Oxford in the 1920s where he managed the shop belonging to David Druce in St Ebbes. About 1930 he started his own business at 3 Cowley Road; the shop was fitted out by A. J. Pye and this was their first building project after the business was established at Kennington.

Harry was joined by his son Bernard H. Slater after the 2nd World War and the business continued as a valuable source of high quality fresh fish, poultry and game until March 1983 when Bernard retired.

Slater's was the first shop in Oxford to produce ice on the premises; previously ice had been obtained from the Oxford Cold Stores in Park End Street, which not only supplied ice to retailers but would store produce in their ice houses. Just after the war a machine was installed which was purchased from Alden's Heating Engineering Co. in New Road.

One of the fleet of Slater's delivery vans, which were used to supply schools, hotels, colleges and businesses throughout the area.

Bernard Slater joined his father Harry in the business after the war in 1945. He became Chairman of the Oxford and District Retail Association and represented them at the National Federation of Fishmongers where he was elected to the Executive and Finance Committee. In 1965, he was elected as President and can be seen on the left wearing his medal of office; he continues to be a life vice-president of the National Federation. In the late 1960s, he was instrumental in the foundation of the Institute of Fish and Poultry and became Vice-President. The Institute was formed to raise the status of the trade and membership is obtained by the successful completion of examinations set by this body.

Bernard Slater seen above in 1965 receiving his presidential badge of office from the retiring president, George Hart of Bath, at the annual conference of the National Federation of Fishmongers and Poulterers. The Federation had been formed in 1932 and this conference was held at Weston-Super-Mare and the Mayor of the town can be seen between the two officers.

The Norma Clark School of Dancing

Norma Clark pictured on the right taught tap and ballet dancing on Saturday mornings at the Alma Hall in Alma Place during the 1930s.

The group gave many performances at a variety of local venues including the Town Hall.

MOTHERS' AFTERNOON

NORMA CLARK

presents

HER PUPILS

in

"HAPPY FEET"
(A Dancing Revuette)

AT THE PIANO
MRS. M. SPENTON

4d.

Oliver & Son, Printers, 73 George Street, Oxford.

Doreen Rose was a member of the group and is pictured above in 1938. She is wearing her Miss Vanity costume which is listed as No.8 in the programme. This was part of a programme performed for a Mothers' Afternoon called 'Happy Feet'. Mrs. M. Spenton played the piano and forty separate items were included. Doreen danced in ten of them.

Celebrations

Coronation party Bath Street 1936.

Coronation party Bath Street 1953.

St Clement's celebrate the Coronation of George 5th in 1936 at Tyndale Hall. Among the group are Mrs Bridgwater with Pearl and Basil, Hilda and Jean Wyatt, Ada, Elsie, George and Raymond Hayward with their mother Mrs Annie Hayward, Rose Woodward, Mrs Cook and Barbara Cook.

Coronation Queen Maureen Shepherd, in Bath Street 1953, with her helpers. Left to right: — Jones, —, —, Teresa Simms, —, Gillian Jones, —.

Coronation party in 1953 at the Coach and Horses Public House, St Clements. Most present were residents of Bath Street. The group includes the landlord and landlady, Mr and Mrs Blackford and daughter.

Cowley Road Methodist Church

Wesleyan Methodism in East Oxford dates from 1872. Mr. Walter Slaughter, a young man trained in a Methodist home, gathered together a few boys and started a Sunday school. His meetings were held in a small room over a stable in Chapel Street, Cowley Road, and the numbers increased rapidly. A larger meeting place was found in premises in Alma Place, which had been used by the Primitive Methodists until 1875 when their new chapel was opened in Pembroke Street (Rectory Road)

It was soon obvious that something larger and more permanent was required. A site was acquired in William Street (Tyndale Road) in 1882

Foundation stones were laid on 13th December 1882 and the St. Clements Mission Chapel, as it was then called, was opened on Good Friday 1883 at a cost of £850. The chapel sufficed for twelve years and it was then found necessary to erect an additional school room.

Within ten years even this enlarged building proved inadequate to the growing needs of East Oxford.

Mr. Walter J. Slaughter

The opening ceremony 22nd September 1904.

A decision was taken to build an entirely new, more spacious chapel. A site was obtained in Cowley Road, were the Oxford Co-Operative Society building later stood, but this scheme was eventually abandoned. A new site was obtained from the Donnington Trustees at the corner of Jeune Street and Cowley Road. The foundation stone was laid on Thursday 30th July 1903.

The new Wesley Hall (Architect Steven Salter) built by Messrs Kingerley and Sons was opened on Thursday 22nd September 1904.

On Sunday 23rd September 1910 the Rev. Grainger Hargreaves unveiled a tablet, inside the church, to the memory of Mr. W. Slaughter who died in 1909 aged 55.

In 1932, as a result of the union of Methodist churches, Wesley Hall Methodists were joined by the Primitive Methodists in Pembroke Street (Rectory Road).

Rev. Shirley Herrick
1904-1907

Rev. Henry Buckley
1907-1910

In 1934 the trustees decided to change the name of the church from Wesley Hall to Cowley Road Methodist Church. Finally in 1952 the decision was taken to unite the two congregations in Cowley Road and to close the Pembroke Street Church.

During the first 50 years the church was served by 14 ministers.

Rev. Henry High
1910-1913

Rev. Charles Pengelly
1913-1915

Rev. John Platt
1915-1920

Rev. Edward Gearey
1920-1922

Rev. Alfred Robinson
1922-1925

Rev. Wesley Hickman
1925-1928

Rev. Woodman Treleaven
1928-1931

Rev. Shirley Cumberland
1928-1931

Rev. Hamblin Parsons
1936-1941

Rev. Latimer Hardaker
1941-1946

Rev. Peter Woods
1946-1950

Rev. Herbert Leigh
1950-1955

12th Oxford Troup c1943 including Sea Scouts. Back row: –, –, –, –, J. Newman, –, –, –, J. Bryant, D. Odell, E.Amore, –, – Ducket, C. Croxson, – Maxwell, –, –, – Harvey, – Cosh, – Enoch. Third row: –, –, R. Lincoln, – Viner, R. Hodges, D. Hodges, –, I.Brough, R.Scarret, B.Sturges, –, N.Hodges, –, –, – Armstrong, –, W. Blondeaux, K. Ranklin. Second row: D. Pickwell, D. Quartermain, E. Lambert, L. Drake, –, Rev. L. P. Hardacre, W. G. Gray, S. Wright, A. C. Saw, –, D. Smith, P. Sturges, –, –. Front row: A. White, –, – Goldstein, R. Toms, J. Scoble, – Greenshield, A. Randle, K. Collet, R. Dean, – Margetts, – Evans, – Wells, –, G. White, B. Wells.

In 1922, by the efforts of Mr. W.G.Gray (who remained its faithful Scouter until 1948), a Boy Scout Troup, the 12th Oxford, was formed which was initially sponsored and controlled by the Sunday School, and in 1927 a Girl Guide Company came into existence.

12th Oxford Scout Group c1955. Back Row: –, –, T. Morse, –, –, –,B. Carvell, A. Loveridge, –, D. Skinner, –, D. Wintersgill. Forth Row: N. Smith, R. Harse, D. Vallender, D. Connolly, M. Walton, J. Aikeman, P. Vallender, M. Dent, C. Young, J. Ford, D. Rolls, H. Hardiman. Third Row: D. Whiteman, R. Hilsdon, J. McNaughton, E. Scoble, J. Scoble, Rev. H. Leigh, D. Hodges, B. McNaughton, L. Whitehouse, T. Adams, C. Gammon. Second Row: M. Fisher (3rd left), Peter Goodgame (7th left). Front Row: Peter Biggs (3rd left), Keith Wintersgill (5th right).

Kit Inspection Summer Camp 1958, South Wales. P. Biggs and K. Wintersgill, –, –.

Left to right: I. Smith, L. White-house, N. Edwards, A. Benning, T. Parsons.

12th Oxford Troup c1965. Back Row: G. Pateman, S. Ling, D. Bishop, D. Lardner, M. Egerton, J. Turnbull, R. Andrews, D. Read, M. Darke, C. Read, P. Dally. Fourth Row: D. Northover, M. Varney, A. Bailey, I. Bradbury. Third Row: A. Benning, G. Coleman, J. Townsend, D. Hodges, J. Scoble, C. Gammon, P. Valender, B. Alladyce, P. Townsend, N. Edwards. Second Row: –, P. Bailey, M. Godby, B. Middleton, W. Moses, S. Alcock, M. Hoggett, –, –, –, –. Front Row: L. MacFarlene, –, –, –, –, I. Roberts.

The Sea Scout section had their headquarters in Meadow Lane, near Donnington Bridge

c1947 Left to right: Bob Gurden, Ted Abbey, Jim McNaughton, John Scoble, Garetl Harris, Ken Courtney.

c1948 On the Thames with their boat the Gay Dophin.

The guide section at the Methodist Church was the 5th East Oxford.

c1948 Pulling the treck cart to Whytham for Christmas camp. Left to right: Joan Bell, Dorothy Adams, Nina Phipps, June Higgins, Marion Gammon, Mavis Green, Lorna Stacey.

Miss Molly Axtell District Captain and Leader of the 5th East Oxford guides for many years.

5th East Oxford Brownie Pack started in 1947 by Jean Hodges (centre back row).

The Primitive Methodist chapel

PEMBROKE-STREET CHAPEL, ST. CLEMENT'S, OXFORD.

Primitive Methodists seceded from the main body of Methodism. They built themselves a new chapel in St. Ebbes in 1843 and another in Pembroke Street (Rectory Road) in 1875, designed by J. C. Curtis. The chapel was registered for worship in 1877. The chapel finally closed in 1953 when it was amalgamated with the Jeune Street Methodists.

The last Primitive Methodist Chapel district luncheon at the Pembroke Street Chapel in April 1933.

Scouts and Guides

The 2nd Oxford Boy Scouts and 1st East Oxford Guides at S. S. Mary and John.

Vincent Smart, Scoutmaster 1908-1912.

The scout group originated in 1908, when a group of lads met beside Boundary Brook, where the Donnington Health Centre now stands. They were reading Robert Baden — Powell's book, *Scouting for Boys,* and were fired with enthusiasm for the adventures outlined in the publication. They decided to start their own Scout Group; they had no premises or leader but met in the fields and were allowed to use an old greenhouse at 12 Parker Street during bad weather. They realised that they needed a leader and asked Major James of 131, Divinity Road to fulfil this role. The troop started with 30 boys and the leadership soon transferred to Mr Vincent Smart, who lived at 12 Parker Street. He found them a permanent headquarters in the original East Oxford School in St Mary's Road and after several moves, the troop settled in the Church Hall of S. S. Mary and John.

In 1909 each troop had to register with their Boy Scout Local Association and unfortunately Scoutmaster Smart's was the second application to arrive. He was very disappointed and told the local press, ' *We are the second Oxford Troop but in discipline, in helpfulness and in all that pertains to true Scoutcraft, we will be second to none'.* From then on, the troop motto was 'NULLI SECUNDUS'.

2nd Oxford Scouts 1938. Back row: D. Mitchell, R Weedon, T. Broad, D. Bint (PL), E. Hudson, N. Pavier, F. Hazeldine, F. Wiltshire, J. Wiltshire. 2nd row: R. Howard (PL), W. Barnes (ASM), B. Bint (SM), J. Houghton (RS), C. Pavier (PL), D. Colley (PL). Front row: P. Mitchell, K. Bolton, D. Weedon, A. Hazeldine, L. Norris, R. Durham, J. Sage, G. Durham.

The 2nd Oxford Troop c.1956. Back row: Ray Beale (flag bearer), Barry Beesley, – , –, David Ledger, Roger Arnold (back), Robert Pether, Robin Waite, Tony Ledger, Stephen Bull, rest unknown, Douglas Bradley (flag bearer). Middle row: Robert Smith, Ian Orford, Roger Hall, John Pether, Paul Onions, Peter Valentine, Richard Desborough, Bob Morris, – , –, Wilf Green, Ray Green. Front row: Trevor Herman, Ron Kearley, –, Pat (now Lavis), Mary Parker, Alan Belderson, Reg Hayes, Gert Parker, Ron Green, John East, John Kirby, Dave Green.

The Officers in 1956 outside the church hall. Back row: Ron Green, Michael Faulkner, Trevor Herman, John Kirby, Alan Belderson, David Green, Ron Kearley. Front row: Geoff Parker, Pat Griffin, Reg Hayes, Mary Parker, John East.

On 17 March 1990 there was a celebration in the church hall of S. S. Mary & John to commemorate Reg Hayes fifty years of service to the 2nd Oxford Scout Troop.

A group of 2nd Oxford and Temple Cowley School. Scouts at the Duke of Edinburgh Conference in 1956. Back row: David Childs, Tony Teagle, Douglas Bradley, Philip Drake, –. Middle row: –, Ted Tolputt, Roy Beale. Front row: Brian Yates, Tony Moss, Bob Morris, Mick Moffat, John Dawson.

David Ledger receiving his bushman's thong as part of the Queen's Scout Award in 1960. The thong was presented at the Scout Fete in Hertford Street by a City Councillor and Reg Hayes the Scoutmaster can be seen behind. The scouts are from left to right: Roger Watts, Paul Plucknett, David Stone, –, –.

Senior scouts at camp c1960. Back row: Leo Edwards, Roger Hall, Bob Stewart (Scoutmaster), Nicholas Liddicoat, Chris Chaundey? Front row: David Ledger, Geoff Beesley.

The Gang Show in 1952. Back row: Michael Faulkner, Peter Cundy Tony Goddard, Heather Greenaway, Ron Green, Joan Emery. Middle row: John Hirons, Jennifer Davies, –, Alan Cundy, Don Timms, Joan Morris, Daphne East, –, – Trevena, Malcolm Williams, Tony Tannant, Keith Valentine, – Anderson, – Flooks, John Arnold, John Lillis, Ray Green. Front row: John Pether, –, Roy Beale, –, Roger Arnold, –, –, Brian Copeland, Peter Valentine, –, Alan Bunting, Bill Paine, –, Richard Desborough, Robert Pether, –.

The scouts and guides provided a guard of honour at the wedding of their two leaders in 1962. The bride was Joan Morris of the 1st East Oxford Guides and the groom was Don Timms of the 2nd Oxford Scout Troop. The wedding took place at the church of S.S. Mary and John. Guard of honour were guides, Susan Howells, Valerie Tarrant, −, −, Janet Nixon and scouts, −, −, Fred Sims, Klaus Hodge, Graham Barson, −.

The 1st East Oxford Guides and Brownies on parade in 1958. Back row: −, Carol East, Margaret Desborough, Elaine Wilkinson, Jaqueline Wakefield, Thelma Barratt, Janet Howells, Krystyna Korski, Janet Nixon, Joan Nixon. Middle row: Jane Rideout, Maureen Ford, Lieutenant Joan Morris, Brown Owl Mrs Tarrant, Captain Loelia Lavis, −, Susan Best. Front row: brownies Margaret Griffin, −, S Williams, Susan Knowles, Valerie Tarrant, Helen Welch, Elizabeth Mills, Susan Mills, Geraldine Payne.

Miss Mary Armstrong, District Commissioner for East Oxford held a Camper's Licence, shown on the right, and took the 1st East Oxford Guides camping.

Guides seen at Spelsbury camping in 1955. Back row: Alison Thompson, Claire Burridge, Q. M., Thelma Barrett, Joanne Mardell. Maureen Ford, Captain Miss Mary Armstrong. Kneeling: Jane Sharp, Jane Allnatt. Front row: Janet Howells, Susan Best, Angela Bruce, Daphne East, Pauline Pardy, Diana Verbruggen.

Ditchley Park Jubilee Camp 1960. Back row: Mrs Smith, M. Desborough, D. East, Mr East, Mrs East, J. Howells, J. Holmslowe, –. Middle row: M. James, S. Best, S. Knowles, A. Livingston (Commissioner), Lisbett and Inga Danisgingly, –, C. East, –. Front row: S Brown, D. Trant, R. French, –, –, –, V. Tarrant.

Cowley Road Hospital

The Poor Law Amendment Act 1834 authorised the establishment of parish union workhouses to provide for the poor and infirm. By 1861 the Oxford Workhouse in Wellington Square, which had been established in 1771, was overflowing and the Oxford Poor Law Board ordered that new facilities were to be provided to cater for 330 persons. An 11 acre site was purchased from Magdalen and Pembroke Colleges and designs for the building were invited from Oxford architects.

The winning design was submitted by William Fisher of St Clements. The building was very impressive being constructed of red and white brick and dressed with Bath stone. The foundation stone was laid on 6 April 1863 and the building was ready for use by 1864. It was composed of three sections, one behind the other; the front section housed the elderly and infirm; the central section with the 90 foot tower and weather vane, housed the Master and Matron; the kitchens, dining room, domestic offices and the workshops for the able — bodied were at the rear. A chapel was added in 1865 and an infirmary in 1866 were added almost immediately. (*By kind permission of Building Magazine*)

The regime was severe; the philosophy behind the 1834 Act provided a resource that was *harsh and austere but not ignoble or thoughtless* (W.A.Spooner 1870). The Board of Guardians did not want to make indoor relief more appealing than that which was provided for the independent poor in their own homes. The use of the Workhouse was effectively discouraged yet the need was great; in 1882, between 3000 and 4000 tramps were admitted and in 1908 an incredible 12,450 vagrants are recorded as having spent at least one night at Cowley.

Front Range.

1. Board Room
2. Waiting Room
3 Porter's Rooms
4. Dispensary.
5. Strong Closet.
6. Clothes- store.
7. Drying- room
   for clothing.
8. Tramp's Ward
9. Sick tramp's Ward
10. Probatory Day Rooms.
11.   "   Bedrooms.
12 Cutaneous Diseases
   Ward

Main Building.

13. Master's Sitting Room.
14. Matron's Sitting Room
15. Master's Office
16. Matron's Office
17. Old men & Women's
18 Day Rooms
19 Epileptic Day Rooms
20   "   Bedrooms
21   Able-bodied men &
22   Women's Dayrooms
23
24 Day Nursery
25 Tailor's Shop
26 Shoemakers Shop
27 Married Couples
   Bedroom
28 Married Couples
   Day Room

Offices

29 Wash-house
30 Laundry
31 Drying Room
32 Coal House
33 Brewhouse
34 Oakum
35 Gypsum Pounding
36   "   Store House
37   "   Boiling Room
38 Carpenter's Shop
39 Refactory Cells
40 Dining Hall
41 Steam Cookin
42 Scullery
43 Kitchen
44 Buttery
45 Bread Room
46/ 47 Meat Store
48 Dry Stores
49 Chapel

Infirmary

50 Surgery
51 Nurses Room
52 Sick Ward
53 Convalescent Ward
54/5 Venereal Wards

OXFORD NEW WORKHOUSE.——Ground Plan.

The able-bodied inmates were made to labour in the workshops; they picked oakum which involved pulling old pieces of rope to shreds, which were then used to caulk the gaps between planks on boats. Alternatively, they sieved and bagged up gypsum for plaster work.

The view of Ward B, photographed in 1959 on the right, clearly illustrates the inhospitable interior.

During World War 1, the premises were used by the Cowley section of the Third Southern General Hospital. It provided orthopaedic, surgical and rehabilitation facilities. The headquarters of the hospital was housed in the University Examination School in the High Street.

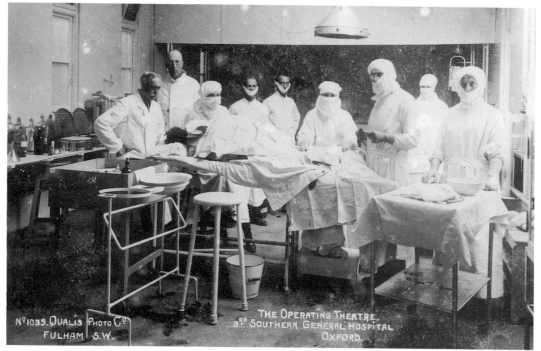

One of the operating theatres in the Third Southern General Hospital, possibly on the Cowley Road site. (*Jeremys PC*)

In 1929, the Local Government Act transferred the management of the Workhouse to the City Council and it became classified as a Public Assistance Institution. It continued to provide for the paupers together with medical, surgical and geriatric cases. Sadly the social stigma attached to the Workhouse resulted in the destruction of all records associated with this era. It is alleged that the documents were burnt in an attempt to remove this stigma.

During World War II, it was used as an Emergency Medical Services Hospital but continued to provide for 220 geriatric patients as well as a 15 bed Maternity Unit. Under the National Health Act 1946, the dilapidated premises were transferred to the Ministry of Health. The post-war years saw an enormous improvement in the care of the elderly and, under the guidance of Dr Cosin, a day hospital and half-way house was set up in the grounds in 1958, for patients to rehabilitate after sickness. Periods of hospitalisation were therefore reduced from over a year to around 35 days. The single storey unit on the right of the drive is called Hurdis House and was named after James Hurdis 1763-1801, Professor of Poetry at Oxford, who happened to live in Temple Cowley.

The Hospital finally closed in 1981 and was subsequently demolished. The geriatric patients were removed to the Radcliffe Infirmary.

Opening of Hurdis House by Edward Kennedy.

An aerial view of the site looking from Morrell Avenue towards the Cowley Road. The East Oxford Health Centre can be seen in front of the Hospital with Hurdis House on the opposite side of the drive. Tuckwells Builders Yard is on the right, the Church of S.S. Mary and John and the Bingo Hall (formerly the Regal Cinema) in the distance with St Bartholomews Chapel and Farm top left.

East Oxford Liberal Club

The inaugural work in connection with the formation of th club was done in the year 1890 and the first annual general meeting was held on January 9th 1891.

Officers elected were: President Mr. C.R. Maltby, Vice Presidents Mr. W. Watts and Mr. C. Moore, Hon. Vice Presidents, Councillors, W.C. Adamson, F.W. Ansell, W.S. Carver, R How, H. James, R. Kempson, W. Rose and G. Wotten. Secretary, Mr. T Coles, Treasurer, Mr. W Richings, Librarian, Mr. John H. Smith. Auditors, Messrs. J. Baker and C. Ewers. Committee, Messrs. E. Jackson, H. Hodges, A. Quelch, W. M. Gray, J. H. Slatter, C. Newman, J. C. Adams, A. Richings, H. Plummer, H. Bennett, T. Byard, A.W. Galpin, W. Hughes, C. Walker(sen), G. C. Burchell.

The club premises were rented, in Crown Street, from the owner, Mr. Carter, but by the end of the first year the club had successfully carried out the purchase. Alterations and improvements were carried out in 1892. In 1897 it was decided to instal incandescent gas lights which remained until electric light was put in during 1905.

Minor alterations were made at regular intervals and in 1902 the club purchased a house in St. Mary's Road next to the club. Mr. Charles Coppock suceeded Mr. H. Bennett as steward at the club in 1904 and he and his wife served the club for many years.

During the two world wars the club did valuable work such as holding concerts to raise funds for war charities, giving entertainment to wounded soldiers and sending parcels to members at the front.

In 1914 the membership stood at 250 but by 1934 it was at its peak of about 600.

Over the years amenities have included, billiards/ snooker,table tennis, darts, shove-halfpenny, cards, library reading room, concerts, whist drives an angling society and a horticultural society.

Although the club gave up its political associations in 1990 and changed its name to The Crown House Club it retains a friendly family atmosphere.

EAST OXFORD LIBERAL CLUB
A Tribute to the sacrifice and service of our members in the world war 1939-1945
To those who fought and nobly fell,
to those who served,they all did well.

Name	Init.	Name	Init.	Name	Init.	Name	Init.
Avery	W.J.	Dickinson	J.R.	Harris	C.E.J.	Robey	F.T.
Allen	L.R.	Deacon	W.K.	Hodgkin	P.B.	Reeve	J.W.
Arnatt	R.W.	Deacon	L.A.	Hobbs	A.	Reeve	A.M.
Archer	C.F	Day	J.A.	Hobbs	C.	Reeve	J.
Adams	A.A.	Day	E.C.	Horsley	N.	Rhymes	H.
Burden	L.G.	Day #	D.D.	James	B.A.	Rhymes	L
Burden	K.E.	Davies	G.N.	James	G.B.	Rogers	E.
Burden	FRED	Davies	L.V.	Johnson	C.R.	Rose	W.R
Burden	F.	Dudgeon	H.J.	Kingswell	E.	Ray	M.
Burden	D.	Earl	J.	Knapp	H.	Smithson	H.L
Baldwin	D.P.	Earl	W.A.	Kempson	R.R.	Surman	J.M.
Brewer	G.E.H.	Earl	H.W.	Knight	R.T.C.	Scragg	F.R.
Bucket	ERIC	Earl	G.	Knight	T.A.	Skinner	E.
Benham	A.A.	East	F.	Keep	C.	Skinner	W.H
Benham	G.	East	C.E.	Lapworth	T.H.	Stoppani	G.E.
Bough	F.H.	East #	A.E.	Laughton	R.F.	Salcombe	G.F.
Barltrop	A.	Eldridge	F.	Lindsey	T.	Saunders	V.C.
Barrett	H.	Eyre	K.	Morriss	W.J.	Tanner	L.H.C
Bateson	J.H.	Eyre	C.	Morris	P.A.E.	Tackley	E.P.
Blunsdon	A.E.	Fortesque	A.R.	Moore	E.C.F.	Tackley	E.W.
Barnes	G.	Flint	L.G.D.	Mills	L	Timbs	F.F.
Butler	G.W.	French	P.	Mackenzie	R.J.	Timms	W.J.
Bestley	D.H.	Gray	P.R.K.	Munn	A.C.	Vallender	W.A.
Chacksfield	R.J.	Gray	V.C.	Nicholls	L.M.	Wakeford	E.
Crapper	S.	Gray	R.M..	Norridge	L.T.	Wakeford	D.
Carter	A.	Goff	H.R.	Norridge	C.	Wale	C.A.
Carter	E.	Green	R.M.	Nash	B.J.	Wall	P.I.
Clack	K.J.	Herbert	R.	Osborne	P.	Way	H.J.
Collett #	A.H.	Head	G.G.	Osborne	G.	Weedon	A.J.
Clack	L.C.	Hunt	R.	Osborne	J.	Wicks	W.E.
Collins	T.J.	Hunt	F.H.	Pipkin	R.J.	Wilks	H.G.
Cosier	R.	Hunt	W.F.	Perkins	L.C.	Wilks	R
Clifford	H.S.	Hay #	C.B.J.	Perkins	R.	Wheeler	S.J.
Coles	J.	Hewer	W.J.	Perkins	E.W.	Willmott	C.
Clarke	W.E.B.	Hewer	J.W.	Pitcher	F.	Webb	G.A.
Cains	C.	Hewer	T.H.	Phipps	G.A.	Wilks	H.
Dubber	F.	Horne	R..	Radford	J.	Whittington	G.

Made the supreme sacrifice

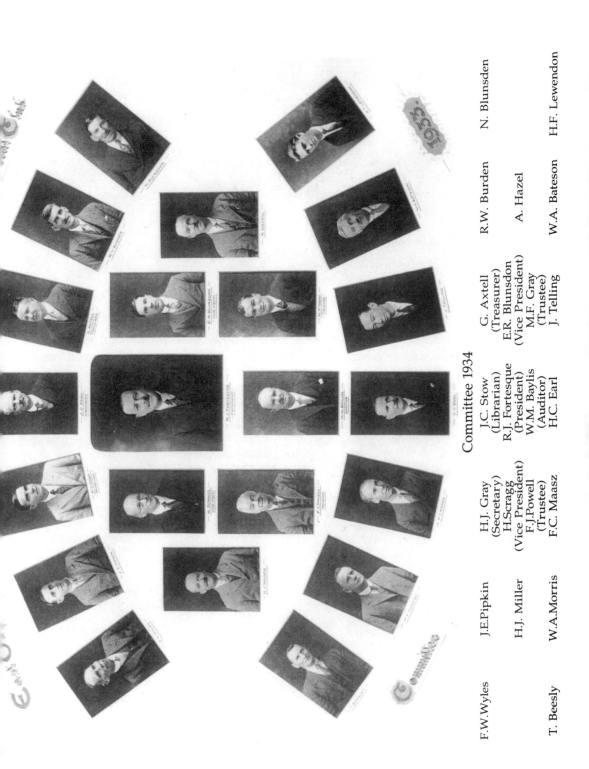

Committee 1934

F.W.Wyles	J.E.Pipkin	
	H.J. Miller	
T. Beesly	W.A.Morris	

J.C. Stow (Librarian)
R.J. Fortesque (President)
W.M. Baylis (Auditor)
H.C. Earl

H.J. Gray (Secretary)
H.Scragg (Vice President)
F.J.Powell (Trustee)
F.C. Maasz

G. Axtell (Treasurer)
E.R. Blunsdon (Vice President)
M.F. Gray (Trustee)
J. Telling

R.W. Burden   N. Blunsden

A. Hazel

W.A. Bateson   H.F. Lewendon

Onions raffled for the servicemens comforts fund. Bill Osborne (monumental mason from Hurst Street) and Alf. Wakefield. c1941.

Members of the horticulture section with their prize exhibits. c1944. Left to right: Bill Bateson, Alf Pipkin, Tom Knight(at back), competition judge?, Ernie Lloyd, Reg Fortesque, Mr. Parker? (judge), Fred. Trafford, Alf Wakefield.

Winners of the Oxford league handicap Table Tennis championship 1947-1948. Back row: R. Hunt D. Banton. Front row: C. Head F. Timbs (Captain), R. Reeve. On their way to the championship they had victories over: Radiators B 13-3, Y.M.C.A. A 13-6, Morris Motors A 16-6, Univ. Press A 13-10 and Pressed Steel A 13-7.

The City of Oxford Motor Services

Leopold Street was the main depot and stabling for the City of Oxford and District Tramways Company, which operated a fleet of horse — drawn trams and provided transport for up to 50,000 passengers per year from 1881. The Cowley branch ran over Magdalen Bridge, which had to be widened to accommodate the 4 foot gauge track, then on to Carfax, and the railway station. At one time, the depot provided 17 tramcars pulled by 130 horses; the maximum speed was 8 miles per hour and the service ran regularly at 15 minute intervals! The carriages were red and white and seated 24 passengers. Double decker trams were introduced in March 1882.

A horse-drawn tram.

By 1900, electric trams were being used successfully in other cities, and a company was formed in Oxford to establish the system. However it was rejected in favour of motor buses as the overhead wires were deemed unsightly. William Morris had started his own private bus service in competition with the Tram Company but gave up his licence in January 1914, and for the next seven years, motor buses were run by the Oxford Electric Tram Company. The City of Oxford Motor Services Ltd was formed in 1921.

A double decker motor bus standing at the terminus outside the University and City Arms in Magdalen Road c.1915. The motor buses had replaced the horse-drawn trams two years before in 1913.

Ancient and modern buses at the junction of Cowley Road and Southfield Road c.1913

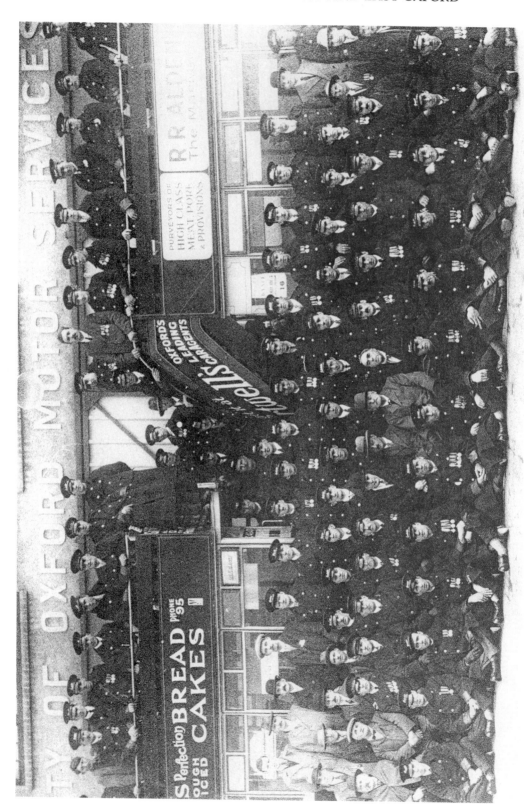

The City of Oxford Motor Services employees at the Cowley Road Garage in 1928. (*O.P.A.*)

Oxford bus at the bottom of Divinity Road in July 1966. The No 1 service had been extended to Littlemore, Florence Park and Blackbird Leys by this date.

The City of Oxford Motor Services Office Christmas party c1960. Left to right: Sheila Dixon, Rosemary Dowle, Gloria Howkins, Ron — (back), Janet Hickman, Lorna —, —, Edna Chowing (front), —.

Ada Hayward pictured c.1955, served as a bus conductress for over ten years, from the early 1950s to 1963. Until 1961 she worked on the No 2 route, which ran, as it does today, from North Oxford to Headington.

John McCabe on the left above was a bus driver on the No 2 route. He started his career in St Andrews in Scotland and came to Oxford in the early 1950s.

John and Ada worked well as a team, at a time when the driver was in his cab and needed a conductress to take the fares and oversee the passengers.

John Mccabe married Ada Hayward at St Clement's Church on 15 August 1958. In 1963, Ada left the Company to have their daughter Sheila.

The Advance Laundry

The laundry was established on the site of the Oxford City Tram Depot in Leopold Street in 1927, when the Bus Company removed to the larger Cowley Road site.

Packing the clean laundry in the 1960s. In the centre facing us is Mrs Win Dowle.

The Advance Laundry packers Christmas Party in the 1960s. Kath —, Carol Woodstock, Lil —, Win Dowle, Dora —.

Local Personalities

Thomas Stone was a tailor who worked from his home at 76 East Avenue. He had been apprenticed somewhere in the city and started his business in East Oxford after the 1st World war. He is pictured on the right with his two grandsons, Wally King (left) and Ralph King (right) outside 80 East Avenue. Thomas Stone was also a life member of the Oxford City Athletic Club.

Rosemary Beadle outside her home at 22 East Avenue. She was the youngest child of Albert and Ivy Beadle, who came from Gosport. Albert had served in the Royal Marines and came to Oxford to work at The Poplars — the Poor Law Industrial School at Cowley. Their three children, Arthur, Norman and Rosemary were all born in Oxford. The family resided at this address from 1928-39.

Alfred Izzard and Family.

Alfred was the son of Henry and Hannah Izzard who came from Spitalfields in the 1860s and lived at 115 Magdalen Road, where he is listed as a Grocer and General Dealer. Alfred was well known in East Oxford; he had a variety of occupations — hawker, paper mill worker and more famously, jockey. He raced abroad as well as in this country and was friendly with the famous jockey, Fred Archer.

Alfred married Rosetta Ann Ludlow from Iffley in 1881; they lived at 82 Catherine Street and had 7 children. The eldest was Thomas Henry who died in 1918 of wounds incurred in the war. He is buried in France and tragically, Rosetta died 4 months later of a broken heart.

Thomas Henry, Rosetta and Alfred Izzard during W.W.I.

Alfred Izzard in his jockey's silks c.1900 above left, and in later life above right on the Cowley Road waving his cane. Everyone knew Alfred in his later years, as he could be seen daily walking from his home to Carfax and back. On one such journey he collapsed and died in Mr Hatt, the butcher's yard at 184 Cowley Road. It was 24 November 1933 and he was 77 years old. Two of his sons followed him and became jockeys, Herbert James and Alfred Stephen George. Both rode internationally and rode together whenever possible; they died within months of each other in 1960.

Joseph Henry Morris, Master Plumber

Joseph was born in Jericho and married Lilian from Holywell in 1933. They then took up residence at 24 Cowley Road near the Plain. He was a self employed master plumber and often worked for

J. Dean & Son at 23-23A Cowley Road opposite his home. He had six children, Tony, Michael, Pamela, Joan, David and Alan and he lived at No 24 until he died in 1968. Lilian his wife, remained until she reached the age of 82 years in 1984.

Joan, Pam, Lilian and Joseph Morris outside the Jeune Street Methodist Church c. 1960.

William Bradley, Electrician

The Bradley family of 144 Hurst Street, at the christening of their 4th and youngest child David, in July 1957 at S.S. Mary and John. Bill Bradley and Vera, his wife, came from Caerphilly in South Wales. Bill, an electrician, arrived in 1934 and Vera in 1935; they met in Oxford and married. Left to right: Bill Bradley, Tom Williams, Vera Bradley, —, Pamela Bradley holding baby David, Kit Evans, Ronald Hurst, Blodwen Bradley, Doris Williams, Sybil Hurst, Jack Evans, Evelyn Bradley and in the front: Jennifer Williams and Roger Bradley.

Tyndale Baby Clinic

Nurse Smith at the Baby Clinic in the hall in 1935.

Celebrations

V.J. Day party Cricket Road.

V.E. party Percy Street.

V. J. Day celebrations. Residents, families and friends. Numbers 92 to 112 Cricket Road. Back Row: −, Mrs. Talboys, −, −, Mrs. Hookham, −, −, Mrs. Lenthall, Mrs. Gable, Mrs. Higgins. Third Row: Mrs. Watson snr, Mr. Gammon, Mr. Varney, Marcia Hall, Margaret Talboys, Joyce Lenthall, June Higgins, Elaine Bough, −, Mrs. Ayres?, Mrs. Lark?, Mr. Higgins, Mrs Gammon. Second Row: Marion Gammon, Irene Lenthall, Pam Ayris, Colin Gammon, Ann Lark, −, Peter Hookham, Michael Ayris, Mrs. Page, Mrs. Burden. Front row: −, Mrs. Varney, Michael Varney, David Varney, Carol Watson, −, Suzanne Gammon, −, Derek Rolls, Graham Rolls, Mrs. Rolls, Mrs. Watson. As the party was held mid afternoon many fathers and older brothers would have been at work.

Coronation party fancy dress Cricket Road 1953.

Coronation party Cricket Road 1953.

Coronation party and entertainment at the Eagle Tavern for the children of Magdalen Road 1953.

V.E. day party at the Donnington Arms for the children of Silver Road, Barnet Street and Howard Street.

V.E. day fancy dress party held at East Oxford School.

V.E. day adult fancy dress/bonnet parade outside East Oxford School.

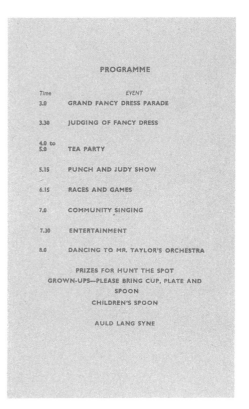

St. Mary's Road Coronation party programme 1953.

St. Mary's Road Coronation day fancy dress parade 1953.

St. Mary's Road fancy dress judging 1953.

Guy Fawkes Night c1915. The Williams children taken at 44 Hertford Street.

Childrens Party Percy Street c 1953

Wedding celebration of Mabel Laura Blaygrove and Harry Perry in Bullingdon Road 26th December 1913. Front row: Bessie Elizabeth Rose Perry (sister) William Perry (father), Rose Perry (mother), Harry Perry, Mabel Laura Blaygrove, Charlotte Ann Blaygrove (mother), Frances James Blaygrove (father), Lily May Blaygrove (sister).

James Street Coronation Party June 1953

The party was to be held in James Street, but in the morning it was raining so it was transferred to the Oxford University rugby ground on the Iffley Road. It was organised by a committee led by Mr and Mrs Mills, who raised about £40.

The three-tier cake, was cut by the oldest James Street resident, Mr Ferris aged 80. The celebrations consisted of a fancy dress parade, sports, community singing, games dancing and a firework display. Each child received a Coronation souvenir and a certificate.

Mary Verbruggen remembers the event:

'In our street was a retired baker, who kindly said, "get me the ingredients and I would love to make a cake." . . . we were still on food rationing and there was one thing the committee could not get and that was dried fruit. So the following days were spent, armed with a basket and paper bag, knocking on everyone's door and asking for a handful of dried fruit. The response was overwhelming and I had to return several times because my basket was so heavy.'

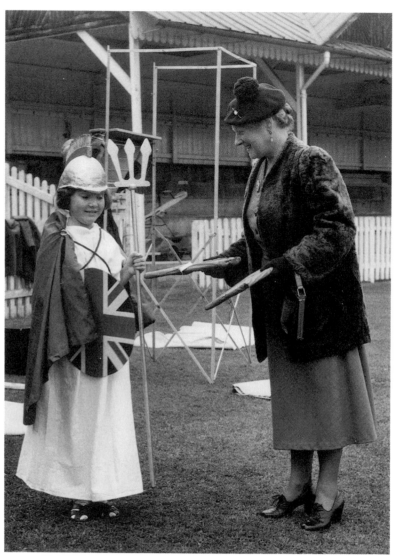

"What should I dress my daughter in for the fancy dress ? Finally, we decided on Rule Britannia, an old sheet was cut up and made into a robe, and with much mess of water and newspaper, the head – dress was moulded of paper mache, the shield of Hardboard and all duly painted." Diana Verbruggen won first prize and is pictured above receiving her award from the local Doctor's wife. Other prize winners were Suzanne Mills, Julie Webster, David Rymes, Keith Buckingham, Terence Morris, Alan Andrews and Dany Mater.

"There were other things to do. My front garden was planted with red salvias, white marguerites and blue lobelia and hung between the two bedroom windows was a large Union Jack.

The Coronation Day arrived and we had a house full of people all anxious to sit all day round our nine inch screen, so with the old black out up at the windows, we spent the day glued to the box. There was Richard Dimbleby giving his unforgetable account of the ceremony and what wonderful pictures, but compared to today what great advancement has been made in television."

Sports and Leisure

The Public Houses were the centre of leisure activities before the days when people had their own cars. Community parties and outings were organised for the locals and their families.

A fishing trip for the men, organised from the Prince of Wales in Charles Street in the early 1930s. Participants are from the left — 1st Mr Frouse, 3rd Eric Perkins, 4th to the rear Sid Eeley and 5th Ed Smith. The rest are unknown. They appear to be standing somewhere near Boundary Brook on the Marsh.

A children's fishing trip, also organised from the Prince of Wales c.1936. Among the group are the Perkins family — Sheila front left, Maria 3rd back, Kath 5th back and Roy at the back of the group on the right.

Outside the Eagle Tavern in Hurst Street on a Sunday morning after sharing a pint with friends in the 1950s. From the left: −, Dai Davies, Bill Bradley, −, −.

Members of the 'Shilling Club' from the Eagle Tavern at the Shillingford Bridge Hotel in 1956. The members collected a shilling at intervals and the fund paid for outings of which this was the first. They felt that the venue was appropriate considering the name of the club. The members are Bill Bradley, Vera Bradley, Bert Douglas, Dot Douglas, −, −, and they all lived in Leopold Street.

A meeting of the 'Shilling Club' in the lounge bar of the Eagle Tavern in Hurst Street c.1959. Back row: Bert Douglas, –, –, –, Cyril Collett, Ted Holland, Doug Wright (landlord) right. Front row: –, Bill Bradley, rest unknown.

The British Legion poppy sellers of East Oxford c1960, gathered in Pembroke Street, now Rectory Road, in preparation for a coach outing to Richmond. They visited the factory where the poppies were made. Vera and Bill Bradley are at the back, to the right of the coach.

Cowley St. John Cricket Tennis and Bowls Club

On Saturday 25th June 1887 the Clergymen and parishioners of Cowley St. John held a meeting to discuss the cricket club. Rev. Walter Scott was in the chair and he was elected as president. James King became Vice President and the strong parochial linkwas emphasised by the appointment of other officers, Rev. Harry S. Carpenter as secretary and Rev. A. Holland as treasurer.

Practice began within a week using equipment purchased by the club from the entrance fee of 6d. There was no permanent captain, the position being selected match by match. Anyone failing to pay their monthly subscription of 6d. forfeited their privileges of membership. Matches in the first season were played on local grounds and of the twelve games played four were won and eight lost.

Headington Quarry C.C.		_Cowley St. John C.C._	
V.J.F. Haden, Esq. not out	110	Rev. H.S. Carpenter, b Stephens	1
D. Stephens, c Tanner, b Franklin	18	A.B. Stocklan, b Botterhill	2
M. Cox, c Bennett, b Tanner	3	H. Bennett, b Stevens	0
G. Hedges, c Franklin, b Tanner	21	F. Tanner, not out	2
F. Botterill, c Franklin, b Tanner	0	G. Franklin	
G. Currill, hit wicket	32	P. Bond	
W. Goodgame, c and b Tanner	0	H. Franklin	
G. Trafford, b Tanner	0	A. Johnson	
J. Coppock, c Johnson, b Tanner	6	P. Shirley	
T. Trafford, b Tanner	4	T. Skerry	
W, Coppock, b Franklin	3	H. Slatter	
Extras	8	Extras	2
Total	205	Total for 3 wickets	7

First score card of a Cowley St. John match away to Headington Quarry Cricket Club. It must be remembered that declarations were unknown until three years later so the home side batted nearly all afternoon for 202 leaving Cowley St. John time to reach 7 for 3.

Mr. Frank J. Fowler,
President 1926-1966

In 1888 the clubs first hat-trick was recorded by F.G. Tanner against the Y.M.C.A. and later during this second season Cowley St. John amalgamated with the Cowley Road United C.C. This increased the playing strength to 38 and two sides were fielded.

The following season F.G. Tanner continued to shine, scoring the clubs first century, 129 not out against United College Servents and was made the club's first captain.

In 1889 the club took a tenancy of the Magdalen ground and they continued to flourish. In 1896 bowls was first discussed and a set of woods was purchased. Three years later it was decided to play tennis. The club now had 118 playing and 50 honorary members.

In 1829 Cowley St. John claimed their first trophy beating Clarendon Press to win the Airey Cup. 1902 saw a move to the Oriel ground and for post match celebrations the club used the nearby University and City Arms public house.

By 1909 membership of the club had grown to 210, 97 cricketers, 65 tennis players and 49 honorary members.

In 1913 the club began a long tenancy of Lincoln College ground and that year the club became known as Cowley St. John Cricket, Tennis and Bowls Club, with the bowls club having a new green laid at Lincoln.

Cowley St. John Cricket Club got stronger as the years progressed and for many years dominated the local scene, providing many players for the county side.

When league cricket made a return for the top local sides, they were always amongst the front runners.In the early 1920s the team became known as The Jacks.

The bowls and tennis sections folded in the early 1980s, while the cricket section amalgamated with Headington C.C. in 1993 to form Oxford C.C.

c1907 Cowley St John Cricket and Lawn Tennis Club.

Cowley St John winners of the Amos George Cup 1947. Their opponents were O.U.P. Jacks players named, Back row: −, S.E. Oswin, H. Parry, −, −, M. Morbey, −, M. Pargeter, P.M. Stone. Second row: P.D. Harrison, −, N. Staples, Alan Dodson (O.U.P), D. Banton, −, M. Piper, −, P. Honour. Front Row: J. Lewis, −, Tony Hopcraft (O.U.P), −.

c1954 Winners of the Jack Young six-a-side. Standing: K. Talboys, G.W. Hopkins, D. Laitt, K. Glover, P. Harrison. Seated: Mr F.J. Fowler (President), D. (Joe) Banton (Captain), Mrs Banton (Scorer).

President F.J. Fowler presents Horace Pocock with a tankard on his retirement after 25 years as club umpire c1955.

The 'Jacks' became the first winners of the Oxfordshire Knock-Out Cup in 1978. Captain Joe Banton receives the trophy.

Keith Talboys, 1948-68

M	I	NO	Runs	Aver
98	169	12	3762	23.96

Joe Banton, 1950-73

M	I	NO	Runs	Aver
208	294	57	5092	21.49

Overs	Mds	Runs	Wks	Aver
4855	1365	12160	571	21.30

David Laitt, 1952-72

M	I	NO	Runs	Aver
140	182	37	1928	13.30

Overs	Mds	Runs	Wks	Aver
4288	1421	1001	670	14.95

Peter Smith, 1963-77

M	I	NO	Runs	Aver
127	158	37	1869	15.45

Overs	Mds	Runs	Wks	Aver
1573	418	4236	227	18.66

Phil Garner, 1971-94

M	I	NO	Runs	Aver
214	374	51	9527	29.50

Overs	Mds	Runs	Wks	Aver
548	147	1628	64	25.44

Rupert Evans, 1973-

M	I	NO	Runs	Aver
138	125	43	811	9.89

Overs	Mds	Runs	Wks	Aver
3684	978	10309	417	24.72

County career records of prominent cricket members

Bowls Section, Oxford Times Triples Winners 1954

Cowley St John (Winners): D. Pargeter, A.J. Cruse, D.B. Ford and the losers, Banbury Central: T. Whitehorn, E. Hunt, W. Powell.

On their way to victory

Club Badge

Leslie Walker (left) and Jesse Room being congratulated by 91 year old Francis Cooper on 50 years membership of the Cowley St John Club. They joined a distinguished list of members who had completed 50 years: Frank Fowler, Teddie Tobin, Ernie Jackman, Bobbie Owens and Arthur Clinkard.

Tennis Section

Members of the Tennis Section with members of Pressed Steel Company Tennis Section on the opening of the Pressed Steel Company Sports Ground 1953. Standing: Tony Denham, Arthur Saunders, Jim Garley, Win Smith, T.Bennett, −, −, Len Blount, Brenda Hobson, Dennis Parker, David Simms, Fred Clark, −, Avril Tull. Front row: Jack Moss, Gwen Beaumont, Jean Street, Alec Wanless, Nora Moffit, Greta Johnson.

Donnington Arms Public House

Mens Outing c1920

Ladies Outing c1920

Donnington Arms F.C. c1928 who played friendly games against local villages. Left to right: Bill Hicks, Cecil Higgs, Cyril King, Jack Hickman, Cyril Beasley, Buster Jacobs, Monk Brockall, – Foster, Sid French, Crocker Dean, Wally Simms.

Star Public House, Pembroke Street (Rectory Road)

Pub regulars at the skittle ally c1920.

East Oxford Bowls Club

East Oxford Bowls Club was formed in 1919,with many of its founder members being shopkeepers and businessmen from the area. Christchurch College ground became the club's first home and they played there until 1927.The club then rented some land on the Cowley Road from Oriel College, and laid its own green which enabled them to progress on a permanent basis.

When Thursday was early closing day for the majority of the shops in Oxford, the East Oxford bowls green had a busy afternoon catering for its shopkeeper members.

Like many bowls clubs there was always a following of bowlers wives and in 1982, no longer being satisfied with watching, a womens section was formed and became a permanent addition to the club.

1925 County honours. Rink champions: J.G. Darlow(skip), J.O. Rhymes(no 1), W. Hammond(no 2), G. Rhymes(no3). Singles champion: G. Rhymes. Pairs champions: A.E. Allen, J.G. Darlow. Standing left to right: A. Kempin (Hon Sec.), W. Hammond, J.O. Rhymes, A.E. Allen. Seated: G. Rhymes, W.R. Slaughter (President), J.G. Darlow.

1921: Back row: W. Millin, T. Smith, W.R. Slaughter, W.H. Street, J. Mansell, F.E.Dunn, H. Slay, A.Briscoe. Second row: J.T. Jakeman, A. Kempin, T.Ballard, W.R. Osbourne, R. Margetts, W.J.Kempson, J.D.A Bear, M. Edgington, T.Hawes, G, Westell, G. Kingston, H.P. Jarvis. First row: S. Barter, F. Trinder, A.E. Allen, G. Quick, G. Rhymes, E.B. Lewis (President), J.G. Darlow, R. Baxter, H.G. Chamberlain, S.J. Barnett. Front row: W.E. Dore, G. Axtell, N. Harris, F. Powell, – Beck, J. Hawtin.

c1945 Left to right: R. Brough, Matt. Gray, J. Telling. R. Brough: Winner, Scragg Singles Handicap and Matt. Gray Single Woods 1943 and 1944. Matt. Gray: President 1942 and 1943. J.Telling: Winner, Lewis Singles Championship 1942 and 1943, runner-up 1944.

1947, J.G. Darlow: Winner, City of Oxford single handed bowls Challenge Cup.

1969 Golden Jubilee season. Back row: A. Baughan, –, J. Lapworth, S. Hallis, K. Chilton, S. Cross, B. Friend, G. Meadows, B. Halsey, J. Crisp, J. Miller, G. Rivers, W. Linnell. Middle row: A.Hiles (groundsman), J. Lines, B. Pullen, R. Dollery, –, A. Jennings, G. King, –, G. Shaw, –, W.Lay, W. Luckett, P.Cruise. Front row: D. Ford, W. Mullard, F. Hounam, W. Stimpson, L. Kenny, L. Harrison, D. Filer (President), G.Haines, S. Taylor, R. Carter, R. James, D. Langford, E. Dove

Relaying the green in 1955. Members were not satisfied with the standard of the green so they decided, under the guidance of the green keeper, Mr Hiles, to relay the green themselves. They needed to get the job done quickly so floodlights were installed in order that work could proceed in the evenings as well as at weekends.

1985: The President Mr C.W. Hainge congratulating Mr A. Hiles (Green Keeper) on 60 years service to the Club. Soon after this occasion Mr Hiles was resting in an armchair in his groundsman's shed with a cup of tea, when he quietly passed away.

The Magdalen Ground

Magdalen Ground c1830, Cowley Road on the right and the spires of Oxford in the distance.

Oxford University Cricket Club grew from two clubs, Bullingdon Green and the Magdalen Club. Rev. H. Jenkins, Headmaster of Magdalen Choir School handed over part of Cowley Common, which he had annexed for his school as a cricket ground. The Magdalen ground was on the Cowley Road (on land bordered now by Magdalen Road and Howard Street) and was the venue for some of the early varsity matches. Oxford University Cricket Club became owners of the ground in 1850, which was the last time the varsity match was played in Oxford, Lords being the venue since then.

OXFORD	First innings		Second innings	
H. E. Knatchbull	b Jenner	7	c Hardy	36
W. M. Musters	st Jenner	29	c Ellis	24
R. Price	b Pickering	5	b Gordon	2
F. L. Popham	c Horsman	22	st Jenner	6
F. B. Wright	c Merryweather	5	st Jenner	27
Chas. Wordsworth	b Jenner	0	b Merryweather	0
C. H. Bayly	b Jenner	0	c Gordon	12
J. C. Robertson	b Jenner	0	not out	10
H. Denison	c Grazebrook	16	b Pickering	18
J. W. Bird	b Pickering	18	bMerryweather	3
J. Cooke	not out	10	c St. John	0
Extras		17		20
	Total	129	Total	158
CAMBRIDGE				
C. H. Jenner	c Price	2	c Wordsworth	12
S Winthrop	b Price	24	b Price	2
H. G. Grazebrook	c Wordsworth	0	b Price	24
E. H. Pickering	run out	2	b Price	14
C. K. Sivewright	c Knatchbull	16	c Bird	13
Hon. F. A. Gordon	run out	7	run out	1
E. Horsman	c Wright	1	not out	0
E. C. Ellis	b Wordsworth	0	b Price	0
W.S.T. Merryweather	not out	20	b Wordsworth	0
E. St. John	b Price	9	c Knatchbull	0
J. R. Hardy	b Price	8	run out	8
Extras		7		2
	Total	96	Total	76

The scorecard from the first varsity match played on the Magdalen ground 1829 Oxford winning by 115 runs.

Schools

The information in this section supplements that in Book One

East Oxford School

Infants in Autumn 1930. Back row: Robin Hemp, Peter Skuce, Basil White, John Lewendon, Leslie Smith, Maurice Smith, —, Desmond Slay. 4th row: Pearl Masters, —, —, Fred Scragg, —, Ted Giles, Richard France, Donald McKenzie, Denis Stone, Maurice Smith, — Curtis, —, —, —, Beryl Allington. 3rd row: Maude Corbin, —, —, Beryl Collins, —, —, —, Rose Walton, 5 unknown, Ruth Church, Dorothy Jennings. 2nd row: —, Nancy Brunsden, Phyllis Sollaway, —, —, —, Pearl —, —, Jean Parker, —, Eileen Evans, Barbara Moss. Front row: —, Richard Goodey, — Bond, —, —, Graeme Sear, — Barnes, Montague Luckett.

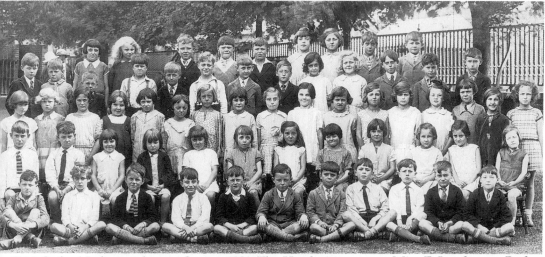

East Oxford Infants taken in Spring 1931. The Headmistress was Miss E. Lambourn. Back row: Antony Edwards? —, —, Patricia —, Peter Stone, —, Reg Earle, —, —, —, Peter Palmer. 4th row: —, — Cox, —, Roy Barrett, Chris Young, Peter Andrews, —, —, —, John Smith, —, —. 3rd row: 4th from left Irene Smith, far right Nancy Woodcock, Dorothy Bell. 2nd row: —, Denis Powell, —, —, —, Thea Pontin? rest unknown. Front row: Maurice Owen, Gordon Rose, Paul Bolton, Douglas Denton, Alan Parker, Leslie Smith, — —, Harold Smart, — Pollard. —, —.

First Year at East Oxford Secondary School in 1947/48. The Head was Mr Martin. Back row: — Trinder, Lewis Cooper, David Hatton, Clifford Healey, Terry Johnson, — King, David Newbiggin, Ronald Tuckwell, Mr Wright. 3rd row — —, —, Donald Taylor, David Cattle, Ronald Lovegrove, David Horn, David Bough, John Stead, Eileen Lewis. 2nd row: Ronald Pringle, 5 unknown, Cicely Bartlett, —, John Gabbitas, Front row: Irene Huish, Rosemary George, Muriel Bookham, —, —, —, Alison Ellsdon.

The May Queen and attendants at East Oxford Secondary Modern School 1961. Anne Walton, June Barnard, Susan Kimber, Wendy — (May Queen), Angela Sherlock, Jane Madden, Susan Morris.

The swimming cup winners in 1953. Back row: John Humphries, Doug Bradley. Middle row: Bill Power, Brian Carpenter, John Lee. Front row: John Ockenden, Richard Masters.

The East Oxford Fancy Dress Competition c1957. Simon Cooper (left) was an icicle, Paul Starkey was a mountaineer, Roger Bradley won 1st prize as a watering can and Maria Kryger was Grandma.

S. S. Mary and John.

The Girls School Staff c1930. Names are amended as they were incorrect in Book One. Back row: Miss Daisy Cowles, Miss Jane Restall, Miss Courtenay, Miss Delamore. Front row: Miss Mott, Mrs Gillett, Miss Nora Seward (Headmistress), –, M. Skinner.

29 May 1953 'A pageant of May-time revels in honour of Queen Elizabeth II. A group of infants are flying their flags.

Miss Thelma Telling's class in 1948. Back row: David Saunders, William Field, Donald French, Helen Fleetwood, John Walker, Jean Knight, Tommy Glanville, Claire Burbidge. 3rd row: Elizabeth Berry, David Cook, Anthony West, Grace Hicks, Richard Holloway, Christine Collier, Alan Munro, Colin Ellis, Lesley James. 2nd row: James Gilfillen, Roy Smith, Leonard Wallbank, Merryl Morgan, Stephanie Downing, Pamela Stevenson, Pamela Earl, Rosemary King, Norma Miller. Front row: John Richards, Robert Adams, Keith Waller, Stephen Purves, Marion Peck, Diana McMichael, David Capar, Michael Rolfe.

The top junior boys class in 1949-50 which was the last year of single sex education. Back row: Mr. Harwood, – Evans, Patrick Mower, Gordon Russell, John Blakeman, Terry Gardiner, Derek Hacket, Tony Belcher, James Bumpas, Keith Joshua, Mr Welsh. Middle row: –, – Ayres, – Scott, Colin Gammon, Christopher Dashfield, – Robinson, – Cundy, – Grant, Donald Timms, Stephen Ward. Front row: – Williams, – Phillips, Paul Smith, –, Peter Green, Terry Padmore, – Bonney, Terry Langstone, – Faulkener.

The Festival of Britain Pageant in 1951. Back row: − Humphries, −, Christopher Chaundey, − Coles, Robert McMinn, −, −, −, −. 3rd row: Sylvia Radburn, Hazel Beesley, −, − Pipkin, June Rollo, −, −, Patricia Burnden. 2nd row: Alan Hemmings, −, David Bates, −, Humphries, −, Michael Pipkin, −. Front row: −, Sheila Parlett, 4 unknown, Christine Clark, −.

S.S. Mary and John Maxwell House football team 1955. Back row: −, Alan Morris, Michael Wilding, −, Wilf Green. Front row: Geoff East, Peter Winkfield, Martin Hooper, Alan Bunting, Robert Foster, Gerald Wiblin.

Southfield Grammar School.

A Grammar School group in 1949/50. Back row: P. Lehburger, J. Gray, J. Hutson, P. Hayle, P.G. Ball, M. Gordon, W. Afford. Middle row: P. Cook, M. Alsworth, I. Parker, P. Read, T. Lindford, P. Hilsdon, A. Hughes, R. Eggleton, J. Diamond. Front row: B. Freeman, D. Saville, P. King, R. J. Thornton, Mr N. C. Teasdale, D. Kerrison, B. Hedge, K. Spicer, R. Preece.

Southfield School 1952. (Surnames only) Back row: Boyle, Freeman, Job, Cundy, Dillon, Scott, Lincoln. 3rd row: Gammon, Blakeman, Hobbs, Timms, Dunford, Lodge, Payne, Heard, Dossett, Chelford. 2nd row: Raiswell, West, Chapple, Gilmore, Bowerman, Burton, Stannard, Buckingham, Flook. Front row: Morley, Mettem, Smith, Horton, Mr Kohler, Girdler, Anderson, Souch, Cooper.

The First Rugby 15 in 1946. Back row: Mick Blake, John Rolfe, Brian Draper, Michael Spira, Mr N.C. Teasdale, Bob Haynes, Ted Baker, Brian Hathaway, Mick Tyler. Middle row: David Dennis, Sam Hignell, Alan Rosser, John Webb, Dennis Banton. Front row: Geoff Walker, Ken Wood (later Mobley).

Southfield Rugby team 1949/50. Back row: Bowley, King, Lindford, Pike, Boyt, Rexworthy, Gray, Jocelyn. Middle row: Clifford, Hutton, Taylor, Romain, Gardiner. Front row: Kerrison, Afford.